TABLE OF CONTENTS

D1456471

From the fullness of his grace we have all received one blessing after another (1:16).

—— 1 ——
The Good News—Fullness of His Grace
John 1:1–2:11

DIMENSION ONE: WHAT DOES THE BIBLE SAY?

Answer these questions by reading John 1

1. What words of Genesis do the first three words of John's Gospel recall? (1:1; Genesis 1:1)

2. What words of John suggest Jesus' divine nature? (1:2-4)

3. What does John tell us about the relationship between life and light, light and darkness? (1:4-5)

4. Who is introduced into the Prologue of the Gospel in 1:6?

5. What is John's purpose? (1:7-8)

6. To whom did the true light come? (1:11)

7. What was given to those who believed and did receive him? (1:12-13)

8. What did the people ("we all") receive in the coming of the Son? (1:16-17)

9. How does John's Gospel describe John the Baptist? (1:23)

10. Where is John baptizing? (1:28)

11. How does John say that he recognized Jesus? (1:32)

12. Who are Jesus' first disciples, as listed by our writer? (1:40-51)

13. Who attended the marriage feast at Cana in Galilee? (2:1-2)

14. What did Jesus say to the servants? (2:7-8)

15. What did the master of the banquet say about the wine? (2:10)

16. What did Jesus achieve by the first of his "signs"? (2:11)

DIMENSION TWO:
WHAT DOES THE BIBLE MEAN?

❏ *John's Gospel Confronts Us Today.* Whatever our situation in life, whatever our perplexities and doubts, our anxieties and sufferings, our triumphs and joys, God confronts us today in the Fourth Gospel. John's Gospel is the story of the divine-human Redeemer. Consider some words from John's Gospel that are fixed in our memories, memories on which we may often dwell:

> *In the beginning was the Word, and the Word was with God, and the Word was God. . . . In him was life, and that life was the light of men. . . . The Word became flesh and made his dwelling among us. We have seen his glory, the glory of the One and Only, who came from the Father, full of grace and truth. . . . No one has ever seen God, but God the One and Only, who is at the Father's side, has made him known* (1:1, 4, 14, 18).

For God so loved the world that he gave his one and only Son, that whoever believes in him shall not perish but have eternal life (3:16).

A new command I give you: Love one another (13:34).

Do not let your hearts be troubled. Trust in God; trust also in me (14:1).

Peace I leave with you; my peace I give you (14:27).

But take heart! I have overcome the world (16:33c).

I am the resurrection and the life. He who believes in me will live, even though he dies (11:25).

These verses and many others in the Gospel express what has happened and what is happening now. Jesus' words and John's words about him describe real events in human experience. When John writes, "I will not leave you as orphans; I will come to you" (14:18), the Fourth Gospel writer is recording a promise that has already been realized.

Who wrote the Gospel? Traditionally the church has attributed the writing to John the son of Zebedee, but no one can be sure that the beloved disciple wrote the book. For generations scholars have researched this question and have developed many theories. The answer still eludes them. Most scholars, I think, would say the Gospel was written around A.D. 85–95. While speculations on authorship and place of writing are interesting and important, most of us are more concerned with asking: What is the meaning of the Fourth Gospel for us?

We are more certain about the people for whom the Gospel was written. These people included members of the church, persons who had come out of Judaism and were immersed in Jewish faith and practice. The Gospel was also written for Greek-speaking Christians of the Mediterranean world, people immersed in Greek thought and culture, and for other people whose cultural traditions were not very binding.

The author focused on the needs of these people of varying cultural backgrounds. He did this so profoundly that he spoke a universal message of God to all times, including our own. He leaves us with the challenge to *believe*—to receive the fullness of the Gospel in our lives and conduct. He tells us that God's unmerited favor (grace) is available to the human race.

❏ *John 1:1-18.* We may call this opening section of the Gospel a prologue, a poem, a preface, or an introduction. The section, written in theological language, unites the whole book. It is a poem with inserted prose comments. Scholars think these verses were a hymn sung by the early church, an adaptation of a Jewish hymn in praise of Wisdom.

More appropriately perhaps, we may see John 1:1-18 as corresponding to the overture or introduction to a great opera or symphony. This overture features themes of life and light and of glory and truth that pervade the Gospel. These themes recur repeatedly, celebrating the grand theme of the Word that exists through all eternity. The Word is pre-existent and incarnate, the revelation of God and the giver of meaning and salvation to God's human children. The Word (Jesus) is of-fered and rejected but stands at last as triumphant over evil and death.

The words *in the beginning* take us to the opening words of Genesis and equate the Word with God. The Word is the eternal, creative, ordering principle that controls all things. "The Word was with God, and the Word was God" (1:1)

John also introduces two other images that pervade the Gospel. These are light and life: "In him was life, and that life was the light of men" (1:4). To be sure, darkness is present, but darkness has never been able to overcome the light. To be sure, also, there have been many witnesses to the light. Evil (darkness) has never been able to overthrow the good (light). What about the light that persists in the Creation? John the Baptist came to bear witness to that light, but he was not himself the light.

Jesus, "the true light that gives light to every man," was coming into the world. Though he was among us and made the world, the world did not know him. He came to his own people—the people chosen by God to achieve God's mission for humankind—and his own people rejected him. John uses the present tense (*shines*), a usage that is in harmony with 1 John 2:8: "The darkness is passing and the true light is already shining." For the Gospel writer the coming of God in the flesh was an event of the past and a gracious promise daily being fulfilled. The darkness represents an attitude in which humankind will not see the light—in other words, a spiritual blindness that rules out the light. In the Prologue and in the rest of the Gospel we find the theme of the portrayal of the struggle between light and darkness. In both the light prevails.

Verses 6-8 are concerned with John the Baptist. We shall discuss these verses later in the context of the relationship between Jesus and John the Baptist.

The hymn in John 1:1-18 celebrates the idea of John 12:46: "I have come into the world as a light." The hymn thus reveals God as the true light that enlightens everyone. Just as the sun's light falls on the just and the unjust, we may assume God's light falls on all whether they admit it or not. The most irresponsible, depraved person in the world is kept alive and sustained daily by God's light.

"The world was made through him" (1:10) represents a return to the theme of the pre-existent Word. This theme counters the false outlook and attitude that rejects the incarnate Son. To believe in Jesus' name means to be identified with him. It means one is divinely recognized when one acknowledges Jesus' claim that he is the Messiah and the Son of God.

Verse 13 emphasizes the need for rebirth. Note the words "children born not of natural descent [in Greek thought the seed of the father was mixed with the blood of the mother], nor of human decision [sexual desire] or a husband's will [human paternity], but born of God." The human being is reborn, born from above. The person is transformed by God's love.

Verses 14 to 18 summarize the theology of the Prologue. They emphasize, as does a great prelude, the meaning of a world symphony. They proclaim the message of the Gospel. "The Word became flesh'—these words stress that God was in God's rightful place when God, in Jesus, lived in our human nature. These words deny the claims of gnostic sects in the Greek world that belittled our human nature and renounced the flesh as in itself evil. These words proclaim the full humanity of Jesus' earthly life. He came and *made his dwelling among us*—that is, the eternal God "pitched his tent" with the human race.

"No one has ever seen God" (1:18). But God has been revealed. We have seen God in Jesus Christ, who is the everlasting demonstration of who God is and what God is like.

❏ *John 1:19-34.* The Prologue to the Gospel of John bears witness to the two natures of Jesus the Christ: He is divine, the eternal Son; he is human, Jesus Christ the Messiah. At the same time in the Prologue, we find that the name of John the Baptist is inserted. The Baptist will testify to the divinity of Jesus. John is presented as "a man who was sent from God," and his testimonies dominate verses 19-34.

The Baptist is the herald who goes before the Messiah proclaiming that the Savior has come. The Baptist sees himself as one involved in the prelude of the great drama of God's salvation. He quickly begins testifying to the One who is greater than he. John reports the Spirit descending like a dove on Jesus, who is proclaimed as the Messiah (1:29-34). John recognizes Jesus as the Son of God, who baptizes with the Holy Spirit.

John asserts that his own ministry is the overture to the great event of God's disclosure. The desert prophet confirms in his words and actions the appearances of the Messiah as they are told in Mark 1:1-11. Mark's tremendous message is, "The time has come. . . . The kingdom of God is near." (1:15). This startling news is conveyed by John the Baptist who affirms: "He must become greater; I must become less" (John 3:30).

❏ *John 1:35-51.* In John's Gospel, Jesus uses the term *Son of Man* (1:51) to affirm his adherence to his ancient religious tradition and to indicate his dignity, mission, and destiny. That is why John placed the title in the "chapter of testimonies," as some scholars refer to this part of the first chapter of John's Gospel.

The "chapter of testimonies" tells of the encounters of Jesus with his future disciples. Here Jesus gathers disciples for his cause. The scenes in which Jesus chooses disciples are prefaced with the great confession of John the Baptist: "Look, the Lamb of God!" (1:36). The lamb is a sacrificial animal, and Jesus comes to be the sacrifice. He gives himself as the sacrifice for us all.

Jesus chooses two disciples from the ranks of John's disciples: Andrew and Andrew's brother Simon (Peter). Then Jesus chooses Philip and Nathanael. The latter is noted for his confession, "Rabbi, you are the Son of God; you are the King of Israel." (1:49).

Jesus chose disciples amid the give-and-take of daily life. The Gospel author describes Jesus as one who led a full human life. John proclaims that God can be known by faith in Jesus Christ, a man who came sharing fully our human life—teaching and serving—one whose love has constituted the movement that we know as the church.

❏ *John 2:1-11.* Jesus is at Cana in Galilee, a community that is friendly to him. He, his mother, and his disciples are attending a wedding party. A joyful occasion, the party has reached "the third day." In those times a marriage feast lasted seven days, and new guests came each succeeding day. In the midst of the merriment the wine supply has become exhausted.

Jesus' mother, knowing of Jesus' willingness and resourcefulness in such situations, senses that Jesus will respond to the human need here. She tells the servants to do whatever Jesus asks. In the interchange with his mother, however, Jesus responds rather sharply. His words to her may be taken as a suggestion not to worry but to wait for the manifestation of God's power. Jesus' hour has not yet come. His words to his mother may also be taken as a reminder that God is at work at the wedding; Jesus knows that a "sign" will be given of God's glory. Finally, Jesus' words may be taken as a rebuke to human arrogance and impatience. We do not determine how God will act. No amount of our calculation, manipulation, or effort can decide the way God's grace will operate.

Jesus rescues the situation at the feast. He directs the servants and brings about the first of the mighty signs that are recorded in the Fourth Gospel. Jesus does not do what others expect of him. He does what he chooses—the divine will. When the wine is brought to the table, the master of the banquet (headwaiter) protests to the bridegroom: "Everyone brings out the choice wine first and then the cheaper wine after the guests have had too much to drink; but you have saved the best till now" (2:10).

The sign is a mighty work that points to the glory and power of God. Its purpose is to strengthen faith.

DIMENSION THREE:
WHAT DOES THE BIBLE MEAN TO ME?

John's Gospel and Us

How have you been confronted by John's Gospel? Quote some of your favorite verses from the Gospel. Recall what prompted them in your mind if you can. What was God saying to you in these verses? How has the Gospel confronted you in particular times of stress and loss? In times of great joy?

What difference do you think the words of the Prologue should make in your search for meaning and value? What does the Prologue tell you about the nature of God? about the nature of God's creation? about the purpose of God for your life? Do you see the universe as ultimately dependable? Why or why not?

What difference does it make to you that John the Baptist is introduced into the Prologue and later discussed in the Gospel? What difference does it make to you whether Jesus is both human and divine? What are John's testimonies concerning the person and work of Jesus? Can you make these same testimonies? Why or why not?

How do you understand the meaning of the "sign" presented in John 2? Does God give us signs today? How can we know they are true? What is John's Gospel saying to you in the story of the wedding feast? What do you think it means for you to "believe in Jesus Christ"?

*For God so loved the world that he gave his
one and only Son, that whoever believes in him
shall not perish but have eternal life (3:16).*

2

Jesus the Savior of the World
John 2:12–4:54

DIMENSION ONE:
WHAT DOES THE BIBLE SAY?

Answer these questions by reading John 2:12-25

1. During what great religious festival does Jesus go up to Jerusalem? (2:13)

2. Who was in the Temple, and what were they doing? (2:14)

3. What does Jesus do and say in the Temple? (2:15-16)

4. What is the response of the Jews, and what is Jesus' answer to them? (2:18-20)

5. What did the disciples finally conclude about the conversation between Jesus and the Jews? (2:21-22)

6. Why does Jesus not trust himself to persons who believe in him because they see the signs that he does? (2:23-25)

Answer these questions by reading John 3

7. What does Nicodemus say first to Jesus? (3:1-2)

8. What does Nicodemus find hard to believe about Jesus' answer? (3:3-4)

9. What is the heart of Jesus' message to Nicodemus? (3:16-21)

10. What is John the Baptist's testimony? (3:25-30)

Answer these questions by reading John 4

11. Whom does Jesus meet at Jacob's well? (4:7)

12. What does the Samaritan woman say when Jesus asks her for a drink? (4:9)

13. What does Jesus tell the woman about the water of life? (4:13-14)

14. What does Jesus say about true worship? (4:21-24)

15. What is said about the Messiah in the conversation? (4:25-26)

16. What is the reaction of the disciples to Jesus' conversation with the woman? (4:27)

17. Who believe in Jesus after the Samaritan woman's testimony? (4:39)

18. What is Jesus' second sign? (4:46-54)

DIMENSION TWO:
WHAT DOES THE BIBLE MEAN?

Each story in this lesson in its own way enhances the main theme of "signs of the kingdom of God." Each points to the universality of the Christian faith.

❏ *John 2:12-15.* During the Passover, Jesus comes to the Temple in Jerusalem. He finds there the money changers at their business and traders who are selling cattle, sheep, and doves for Temple worship.

Making a whip of cords, Jesus drives out the money changers and the traders with their animals. They were defiling the Temple and using religion for their profit. Jesus attacked their system of trade. It was without meaning, a burden on the poor.

Jesus proclaims a new day in religion. The old system of animal sacrifices must give way to an order in which the Temple of wood and stone is replaced by Jesus himself. Jesus will be the living sacrifice. Jesus tells the people involved in the old system, "Destroy this temple, and I will raise it again in three days." Human hands had taken forty-six years to build the Temple, and the Jewish authorities could not see Jesus' meaning. Jesus was speaking of the temple of his body—a new temple to be raised at his resurrection.

Many believed in Jesus when they saw the signs he did. Jesus answers that a faith that depends merely on signs and not on Jesus, the revelation of God, however, is shallow. Faith in signs alone is a shabby faith. Many people were willing to affirm their belief in Jesus as long as the signs were forthcoming, but Jesus refused to trust himself to such people. He knew what is in human beings—our ambiguities, complexities, confusions, and instabilities. He knew our weaknesses that yield to temptations, but he also saw the potential grandeur of the person.

Some people, however, still want a sign. Jesus gives it to them; by his death and resurrection Jesus confronts people with a new reality in religion. His body becomes the new temple. In John 2:19-22 we learn that this new understanding comes after the Resurrection when a new body not made with human hands is raised to take the place of the old Temple.

□ *John 3:1-21.* Nicodemus, "a member of the Jewish ruling council" and a person of wealth, power, and influence, comes to Jesus at night. Nicodemus, a member of the Sanhedrin whose seventy members compose the supreme Jewish legal body of first-century Israel, stands high in Jewish society. He is a Pharisee, a ruler of the Jews, an interpreter of religion and the law, a highly respected teacher of the Jews, an honored official.

Why does Nicodemus visit Jesus at night? This question has intrigued untold numbers of students. Nicodemus may be afraid of community opinion and thus careful not to be seen in the company of Jesus in daylight. Association with this new prophet may have serious consequences. Or Nicodemus may be coming out at night because that is the best time to talk with Jesus. He may want an unhurried, uninterrupted interview; for he has seen how in the daytime Jesus is constantly pressed upon by crowds. Whatever his reasons for coming at night, we should marvel that Nicodemus comes at all.

Nicodemus comes not as one who is merely curious and disinterested. He comes because he has serious questions about the meaning of life and the attainment of truth—the kind of questions we still ask.

Nicodemus has seen Jesus' signs and wonders, and he has been deeply intrigued by these. Jesus tells him that the signs and wonders are not central in his ministry. What is of supreme importance is that a person be transformed by the truth of God—that is, "be born again."

What kind of talk is this? Nicodemus misunderstands Jesus' meaning. In the Greek text the word that Jesus used may mean "from the beginning, completely, radically"; or it may mean "for the second time." The word can also mean "from above" and "from God." Catching up all these meanings, the word describes the transforming grace of God in a human life, for the rebirth or re-creation of the self.

Nicodemus is curious about rebirth. How can it happen? Jesus points out to him the way we experience the wind. We do not know just how the wind blows, but we hear its sounds and see its effects. We do not know how God's grace operates, but we experience its effects. We see what the Spirit does with us and others. An utterly selfish person, obsessed by power-striving, is made into a loving citizen of the Kingdom. A person who is blind to the truth opens his or her mind to it.

We do not know how the discussion between Jesus and Nicodemus ended. Jesus does not tell us. Rather he takes up his own interpretation concerning the discussion. Jesus declares that he came down from heaven to tell us what God is like. Jesus lived among us, died for us, and then returned to God. Jesus is the truth about God.

Then John picks up a story from Numbers 21 to get across his message about Jesus (3:13-14). During their struggle through the desert the Israelites lamented their lot and complained, regretting that they had been released from slavery in Egypt. God rebuked and punished them with a plague of venomous snakes. When the people repented and prayed for God's mercy, Gold told Moses to create an image of the snake and to display it to the people.

Persons who viewed the snake were healed. But the fascinating image of the snake was so powerful that the people worshiped the symbol, not the God to whom the symbol pointed. The rabbis later explained to the people that, not the snake, but God had healed the people. The snake had only been an image to turn their minds to God, the source of all healing power. John used the story to express something of the same truth about Jesus: "Just as Moses lifted up the snake in the desert, so the Son of Man must be lifted up, that everyone who believes in him may have eternal life" (3:14-15).

Then John comes to the heart of Jesus' message: "For God so loved the world. . . ." John proclaims God's purpose to save—the purpose that embraces the whole world, all people of every class and nation and condition.

In Jesus, God came in everlasting mercy, not to condemn the world but to save us. If we believe in Christ (commit our total selves to Christ), we are not condemned; but if we do not do this, we have already condemned ourselves. The light of God's love has come among us; but many of us have loved darkness rather than light, lest our deeds should be exposed. If we do what is true, however, our deeds will come to light; and it will be seen that they have been done in God.

❏ *John 3:22-36.* This section deals with Jesus going to Judea, where John the Baptist is baptizing disciples. John's followers confront John over the genuineness of Jesus' ministry. The Baptist replies that he is only "the friend who attends the bridegroom," who is leading the bride (Israel) to the bridegroom (the Messiah—Jesus).

John chooses this place in his Gospel to testify that Jesus is the authentic spokesman for God. John says that those who believe in Jesus have eternal life. Unbelief is disobedience, and those who do not obey face the wrath of God.

❏ *John 4:1-30, 39-42.* The universal concern and outreach of John's Gospel now begins to unfold with greater rapidity. Jesus, having left Judea, goes away to Galilee, by way of Samaria.

Samaria is a zone where pious Jews do not want to be seen. Jews avoid Samaria when they can, taking the longer road around Samaria rather than traveling through it. The Samaritans are considered a mixed breed, an inferior people. Jews and Samaritans clash over religion. Both groups cherish ancient bitterness and hatred. But directly through Samaria is the shortest route to Galilee from Judea.

Jesus comes to the town of Sychar in Samaria and stops at Jacob's well. Here he asks a Samaritan woman, who arrives "to draw water," for a drink. She is flabbergasted: "You are a Jew and I am a Samaritan woman. How can you ask me for a drink?" How can a Jew abandon his prejudices and taboos to associate with a hated Samaritan? And not only that, the Jew is talking with a woman, asking a favor of her. Jesus is tired and in need of a drink before his disciples return from the town where they have gone to buy food. John's Gospel stresses Jesus' humanity. The Lord of all suffers from hunger and thirst.

How does Jesus respond to the woman's question? He meets her with compassion, kindness, and consideration. He breaks down the social, racial, and religious barriers that have existed for hundreds of years. He treats the Samaritan woman with respect. She is one precious in God's sight. Jesus cuts through the prejudices and low estimates of women that prevail in public, even if she was someone's mother, sister, or wife. Surely, the Samaritan woman thinks, this Jew has taken leave of his senses to violate the taboos against women.

But Jesus listens to the woman's sad story and offers her the water of life. Like Nicodemus, the woman misunderstands Jesus' statement. She takes it in the wrong way. At first she is greatly perplexed. Then she realizes Jesus has lifted the conversation to a higher level. Jesus is offering to her the water of life—salvation, healing, the mercy and loving-kindness of God, life eternal. The woman is, like Nicodemus, confronted with the Savior of the world.

The woman asks Jesus to give her this water. Jesus replies that he wants her to bring her husband to the well. She has no husband, she says; and Jesus agrees. "The man you now have is not your husband."

Suddenly the woman is aware of her sin. In a few words Jesus brings her face to face with reality. She is awakened to her need for God and her need for worship. So she asks Jesus where she can find God. Her ancestors have worshiped God on Mount Gerizim, she says, the sacred spot where Moses first directed an altar to be built in the Promised Land (Deuteronomy 11:29).

Jesus replies that the old religious order, with its old forms and practices, is now abolished. God is not on Mount Gerizim or in Jerusalem. God is everywhere, and true worshipers anywhere can find the God who is worshiped in spirit and in truth. The ancient rivalries and narrow religious affirmations must give way to God, who has opened a new day in religion.

The Samaritan woman is brought to the place where she can see herself. The encounter with Jesus causes her to see herself, and the encounter redeems her life from destruction. It sends her out to tell her neighbors about Jesus. She now lives in love and gratitude.

❑ *John 4:31-38.* The disciples return with food. They urge Jesus to eat something; for he is hungry and exhausted. Jesus replies that his food is to do the will of God, who has sent him into the world. He must finish God's work.

The disciples do not understand Jesus' statement about the food that sustains him. They are thinking of physical hunger. Jesus wants to help them see that his very life is offered to God. He is nourished by the spiritual task God has given him. The Gospel stresses that idea that Jesus is *sent* into the world by God. Jesus must live in perfect obedience to God—that is, God is his food, his sustaining purpose, his source of nourishment.

Then Jesus contemplates in the present situation a vision of the harvest of God being created in the world. When the disciples view the whitening fields, they know that the harvest is near. The sower and the reaper now have their tasks at hand. The reaper will be paid his wages to gather the harvest of eternal life. The sower shares the reaper's joy because his own work has paid off. "One sows and another reaps." Jesus is sending his followers out as reapers. The first fruits of his mission to Samaria are ready to be gathered. Jesus is now sending his disciples out to reap the results of what others have sown.

Jesus is indeed the Savior of the world. His redemptive work reaches out to all peoples.

❏ *John 4:43-54.* John calls this story the "second miraculous sign" that Jesus did in Galilee (4:54). The story illustrates verse 42, where Jesus is seen as the Savior of the world. The healing of the official's son contributes to John's description of the universality of Christianity.

The story is directed at all persons who base their faith on mere signs. The official demands life for his child, not a showy display of magical power. Then he believes Jesus has brought about the cure of his child.

DIMENSION THREE:
WHAT DOES THE BIBLE MEAN TO ME?

A New Day in Religion

John's Gospel confronts modern Christians with a new reality, the universal Savior who brings God's salvation. Faith in Jesus Christ drives out the impediments to life in all its wholeness and gives life a new purpose. How do we experience the new birth? What impediments in your life need to be driven out to achieve God's wholeness?

Jesus comes bringing God's love to humankind. This love shatters the barriers of ignorance, prejudice, selfishness, and hostility. The gospel reaches out to peoples of all classes, races, and nations. Think of your relationships with others. How does prejudice affect your feelings for others? for prisoners? for politicians? for those who do not attend church?

Then Jesus declared, I am the bread of life.
He who comes to me will never go hungry, and he
who believes in me will never be thirsty (6:35).

—— **3** ——
Jesus the Bread of Life
John 5–6

DIMENSION ONE:
WHAT DOES THE BIBLE SAY?

Answer these questions by reading John 5

1. Where does Jesus attend the feast of the Jews? (5:1)

2. What happens at the pool of Bethesda? (5:2-9)

3. How do some Jews respond to Jesus' healing on the sabbath? (5:10, 16)

4. Why do "the Jews" seek all the harder to kill Jesus? (5:18)

5. How does Jesus answer his critics? (5:19-24)

6. What does Jesus say about the coming age? (5:25)

7. Why is Jesus' judgment just? (5:30)

8. What does Jesus say about the witness of John the Baptist? (5:31-36)

9. What witness does Jesus have that he is sent of God? (5:36)

Answer these questions by reading John 6

10. Why does a crowd follow Jesus? (6:2)

11. How do the people respond when they see the sign of the feeding of the five thousand? (6:14)

12. What does Jesus do when he perceives the people want to make him king? (6:15)

13. What does Jesus say to his frightened disciples when they see him walking on the water? (6:20)

14. When the disciples find Jesus on the other side of the lake, what is his response to their questions? (6:26-40)

15. What is the response of "the Jews" to Jesus' words? (6:41-42)

16. How does Jesus answer them? (6:43-51)

17. What is the response of "the Jews" to Jesus' reiteration of his claim? (6:52)

18. How does Jesus answer "the Jews"? (6:53-58)

19. What do the disciples say about Jesus' words? (6:60)

20. What do many of Jesus' disciples do when they hear Jesus' words in verses 61-65? (6:66)

21. What is Peter's confession? (6:68-69)

22. When does Jesus speak of Judas Iscariot? (6:70-71)

DIMENSION TWO:
WHAT DOES THE BIBLE MEAN?

❏ *John 5:1-18.* Jesus came into a setting of misery and desperation. He found a multitude of blind, lame, and paralyzed persons lying at the pool of Bethesda. The scene might resemble a modern hospital shortly after a major disaster. Some individuals were able to reach the pool on their own power and could dive into the water that they believed had healing properties. Others, like the man who was an invalid, were helpless and could find no one to aid them in their efforts to reach the water.

Jesus came into a situation where the need was great. The story indicates how Jesus worked. He opened the encounter with the man by asking the central question: "Do you want to get well?" The question was a way of asking whether the sick man wanted to be fully alive and responsible. The man had been ill for thirty-eight years. Confronted by Jesus, the man answered that he had no one to help him get into the water when it was troubled.

Jesus' question and his summons to life are the same question and challenge he delivers to us. Perhaps the man who was an invalid had become so accustomed to his illness that he used it as an excuse for giving up the struggle. Perhaps he found a certain peace in lying there sick and alone. We who consider ourselves well should not be too hard on such an individual. We know our temptations to evade life.

In the case of this man, Jesus cut through his rationalizations. Did the man want to be wholly alive and responsible for his existence? Then let him pick up his mat and walk. That meant to welcome God's healing power in his life. So confronted, the man was healed. He was ready to be changed.

The healing took place on a sabbath day. This fact raised in superficial minds the issues of what was permissible activity on the sabbath. A man had been cured of a disease that many deemed incurable. The healing should have occasioned rejoicing and thanksgiving, but Jesus' enemies made it into a situation for rancor and bitter debate. Carrying a burden was deemed work. The man's mat was considered a burden, so he

JESUS THE BREAD OF LIFE

was forbidden to carry it on the sabbath. The man, now healed, had broken the law. Jesus had also broken the law. Their violations of the law could have been punishable with death by stoning.

At first the man who had been healed did not know who had healed him. Afterward Jesus found him in the Temple. Jesus said to him, "See, you are well again. Stop sinning or something worse may happen to you" (5:14).

The man now told Jesus' enemies that Jesus had healed him. He did this, not from a desire to hurt Jesus, but to say that it was not his (the healed man's) fault that he had broken the law.

The knowledge that Jesus had healed the sick on the sabbath enraged Jesus' enemies. They turned on Jesus and persecuted him. But Jesus replied to their charge, "My Father is always at his work to this very day, and I, too, am working" (5:17). This response enraged the Jewish leaders even more. Jesus had not only broken the law, he had called God his Father, "making himself equal with God."

Jesus said God did not stop working on the sabbath. Jesus was doing God's work, so he could not stop doing acts of love, mercy, and compassion on the sabbath. Jesus insisted that human need had to take priority over the trivial requirements of the law.

❑ *John 5:19-29.* The distinguished scholar William Barclay has characterized these verses as "The Tremendous Claims" in his translation and interpretation entitled *The Gospel of John* (Revised Edition, Volume 1; The Westminster Press, 1975; pages 184–193). Barclay shows that of all the astonishing claims that Jesus makes the big one is the claim that he is the Son of Man.

Barclay shows that the term *Son of Man* has a long history and originates in Daniel 7:1-14 where Daniel, writing in a time of fierce persecution of the Jews, describes his vision of the terrors that Jews had experienced under the empires that had ruled them. Under the symbolism of beasts, Daniel portrays the empires that have tyrannized Israel. Daniel affirms that these terrible oppressors will cease to be and that power and dominion will be conferred upon "one like the son of man." All this means that the reign of beastly powers will be ended and there will come a power, Barclay writes, "so gentle and kind that it will be human and not bestial" (*The Gospel of John;* page 186). Daniel declares that this loving power will rule the world.

How will this new power be introduced? Barclay maintains that the new age of gentleness, love, and peace will be brought on by a chosen one of God, the Son of Man. The Jews came to call the one to come the "Messiah" or "chosen one." Barclay says the miracle that happened to the paralyzed man (John 5:1-5) was a sign that Jesus was the Son of Man (the Messiah).

Jesus faced the charge that he was making himself equal with God, for in him we see God. How does God react toward sin? How does God feel about us? We look to Jesus and get our answers. Barclay concludes, "The mind of Jesus is the mind of God; the words of Jesus are the words of God; the actions of Jesus are the actions of God" (*The Gospel of John;* page 188).

Jesus' identity with God is based on full obedience. He comes to do, not his own will, but the will of God. So he acts in full confidence that the cause of God will triumph. He is completely fearless.

Barclay points out that John presents three great functions that belong to Jesus Christ in these verses (5:21-23). Jesus is *the giver of life, the bringer of judgment,* and *the receiver of honor.*

Jesus Christ changes our relationship to God. He gives us new life: "No man is fully alive until Jesus Christ enters into him and he enters into Jesus Christ" (*The Gospel of John;* page 189). After this life ends, the person who has accepted Christ inherits life that is still more abundant, "while for the man who had refused Jesus Christ, there comes that death which is separation from God" (*The Gospel of John;* page 189).

❑ *John 5:30-47.* Who and what are Jesus' witnesses that his words are true? His enemies could say that up to now Jesus' own words were all they had to go on. Now Jesus and his foes are in something of a public trial or debate, and Jesus' hearers are demanding evidence—dependable witnesses who will testify that Jesus' words are true. They want proof that he is who he says he is, that his message and his words are the authentic revelation of God. To the Jewish leaders, Jesus is making astonishing claims. Why should anyone believe him?

Jesus asserts that more than the human word is involved in his claims. Always these claims are backed up by divine evidence. He declares again that if he bears witness to himself his testimony is not true: "there is another who testifies in my favor, and I know that his testimony about me is valid" (5:32). God bears witness through the works that Jesus does, and God bears witness through the Scriptures. God demonstrates divine love and salvation through Jesus' works. John the Baptist had testified that Jesus was the Messiah sent by God to take away the sins of the world, but Jesus has a greater witness than John—the mighty work he is doing. God is bearing witness that the work of the Son is genuine.

❏ *John 6:1-15.* This passage gives us the story of the feeding of the five thousand, a miracle that is recorded in all four Gospels (Matthew 14:13-21; Mark 6:32-44; Luke 9:10-17).

The event happens beside the Sea of Tiberias (or Galilee) when Jesus seeks rest from the pressures of the crowds. The people are obviously tired and hungry, but they follow him. To test Philip's faith, Jesus moves to meet their need. Philip declares that two hundred denarii (about eight months' wages) would not buy enough bread (barley loaves, the food of the poor) to feed the multitude. But Jesus feeds them nevertheless. Afterward Jesus asks his followers to gather up the fragments. This act of reverent economy acknowledges God's gift.

The disciples gather up twelve baskets of food. Then the crowds seek to make Jesus king. They want a political messiah who will oppose Rome, but Jesus refuses to be trapped into becoming a secular ruler, into making his kingdom a kingdom of this world.

❏ *John 6:16-21.* We may call this story of Jesus walking on the water or crossing to Capernaum a delightful interlude. The story tells us how Jesus' frightened disciples are calmed by Jesus' calm. His presence makes for serenity amid the strong wind. Jesus is portrayed as "walking on the water," and an air of the miraculous hovers over the story. On the other hand, the Greek words could mean "by the sea." However we interpret the passage, we should not neglect its main lesson: Jesus is greater than any purely human personality; he commands the elements of nature so that his very presence overcomes fear.

❏ *John 6:22-71.* Chapter 6 opens with Jesus providing bread to the multitudes, a fitting symbol of Jesus' concern for helping the people understand the meaning of his ministry. From the beginning, more than bread is involved; for Jesus is thinking of the "sign" that points from the bread the people eat to himself as the bread of heaven. The story develops from Jesus' provision of bread to the giving of the life-sustaining Word from heaven. All human beings yearn for God's bread, a hunger that goes beyond every other hunger.

But here Jesus counters the Tempter's efforts to turn the great hunger into a second-best. Jesus wants to get over to his hearers the message of Matthew 4:4: "Man does not live on bread alone." We are created to live by every word from the mouth of God.

In the memories of the Jews, Moses the prophet had provided bread to famished people in the desert. Jesus sees Moses' deed as a "sign" of a greater time to follow. Jesus, however, identifies his ministry not with Moses but with God who is the real giver of all bread—bread such as God through him has just dispensed and bread from heaven, the bread of eternal life.

DIMENSION THREE:
WHAT DOES THE BIBLE MEAN TO ME?

John 5:1-18—Do I Want to Be Well?

The main question for this lesson becomes: Do I want to be well? Think of some of the rationalizations that the man who was an invalid may have had. Have you been conscious of using such excuses? What maladies do you need relief from? What times in your life have you been aware of God's healing? Are you ready for change?

John 5:19-29—What Does the Messiah Mean to Me?

The Scripture proclaims that the loving power of the Messiah will rule the world. Love will vanquish the beastly powers that torture our world and each of us personally. Are you living as though the Messiah has not come? How does the Messiah summon you to new life? How is Jesus the Messiah the giver of life, the bringer of judgment, the receiver of honor? How do you experience him as the giver of life? How do you know his judgment? How do you honor him? How do you know Jesus is the Messiah?

John 6:1-5—What Does the Feeding of the Multitudes Mean to Me?

Why do you think the story of Jesus' feeding of the crowds is recorded in all four Gospels? What was Jesus saying to you in this story? to the church? to you as a member?

John 6:16-21—Jesus Walking on the Water

What does the story tell you about Jesus' ability to command the forces of nature? What do you learn from it that gives you greater calm in the storms of life?

John 6:22-71—What Does It Mean for Me to Live on the Bread of Life?

What does faith have to do with the bread of life? What does it mean for you to live each day on the bread of life? Do you know eternal life as a gift?

When Jesus spoke again to the people, he said, "I am the light of the world. Whoever follows me will never walk in darkness, but will have the light of life" (8:12).

4

Jesus the Light of the World
John 7–8

DIMENSION ONE:
WHAT DOES THE BIBLE SAY?

Answer these questions by reading John 7

1. Why does Jesus go about in Galilee instead of Judea? (7:1)

2. What do Jesus' brothers tell him to do? (7:3)

3. When Jesus leaves for the Feast and the Jews are looking for him, what do they say? (7:11-12)

4. When Jesus goes into the Temple and teaches, what causes the Jews to be amazed? (7:15)

5. How does Jesus answer them? (7:16-24)

6. How do some of the people of Jerusalem react? (7:25-27)

7. What happens when the Pharisees hear the crowd whispering about Jesus? What is Jesus' response? (7:32-34)

8. What does Jesus do and say on the last day of the Feast? (7:37-39)

9. What happens when the people hear these words? (7:40-44)

10. How is Nicodemus involved in the dispute? (7:50-52)

Answer these questions by reading John 8

11. What happens when Jesus returns to the Temple? (8:1-11)

12. What happens after the incident of the woman taken in adultery? (8:12-30)

13. What does Jesus now say "to the Jews who had believed him"? (8:31-32)

14. How does Jesus answer their assertion that they are free by being "Abraham's descendants"? (8:34-47)

15. How does Jesus answer their insults? (8:49-58)

16. How does this confrontation end? (8:59)

DIMENSION TWO:
WHAT DOES THE BIBLE MEAN?

❑ *John 7:1-13*. What better time for Jesus to make a public demonstration and vindicate his mission to the world! Think of the public relations possibilities! The great national Feast of Tabernacles is coming up. All eyes turn toward Jerusalem, the Holy City.

Jesus' brothers appeal to him to declare himself to the world at this feast. Jesus can verify his claims in Jerusalem (Chapters 5 and 6). Many people are hostile toward him; some are even out to kill him. Perhaps a dramatic and sensational event or sign establishing Jesus' claim will turn the hostile crowd to his side. In a time of great opportunity and danger, the brothers challenge Jesus to show himself. He declines their plea.

His time, or destined hour, has not come, he says. This time will be the hour of God's time, the opportunity when the situation is ripe for achieving God's purposes. If Jesus goes up to Jerusalem now, he says, the time will not be ripe for success in his mission. He will not force God's hand. Reluctant enough to say at first he will not go to Jerusalem at all, Jesus later decides to go there privately. Jesus therefore chooses his own time to visit the Holy City.

What does Jesus find? The Jews are already searching for him. Apparently they expect to hear from him. He is the subject of their discussions. Various Jews are expressing their opinions of Jesus.

Some say he is "a good man," a reaction we often hear today. The world is willing to say nice things about Jesus, but it hesitates when higher claims are made for him. Was he the one he claimed to be? Was he the self-communication of God to the world? Many persons stopped short of affirming this.

Others say no to Jesus, claiming he is deceiving the people. These persons include the Pharisees, the Sadducees, and the chief priests, who hate Jesus because he challenges their trivial rules and regulations. Jesus threatens their false loyalties and complacencies. How dare a lowly Galilean oppose the law!

Summing up the conclusions in Chapter 7 regarding Jesus, we find that (1) he is a good man; (2) he is "the Prophet" (verse 40); (3) he is a brave man; and (4) he is demon-possessed (verse 20). Jesus is alive, a vibrant personality whose presence enlivens every situation. Some people even receive him as the Christ, the anointed of God (verse 41).

❏ *John 7:14-24.* Jesus here seems to continue the argument that appears in Chapter 5. Jesus says again that his teaching comes from God and not from himself.

Jesus is not speaking on his own authority, for to do so would be to seek his own glory. Jesus seeks the glory of God.

Jesus challenges the crowd, asking why they want to kill him. But the people charge him with having a demon. He replies that he did one deed (healed a man on the sabbath), and the people marveled at it. Moses, he says, gave them circumcision (from the fathers); and they circumcise on the sabbath. Why then, if on the sabbath a child receives circumcision so that the Mosaic law may not be broken, are the people angry with him "for healing the whole man on the Sabbath"? Jesus challenges his critics not to be overcome by appearances in their judgment.

❏ *John 7:25-31.* Jesus' teaching leads to a division. One group stands against him because they claim his origin is commonly known. When the Messiah comes, they believe, he will come in mystery. They cannot see why the authorities, who should be aware of the inadequacy in Jesus' background, have failed to follow up on their intention to put him to death. Jesus replies that they know only about his family home on earth. They do not know about his ultimate origin. This is so because they do not know God from whom Jesus has received his commission. They are coming to the dispute with the wrong assumptions.

With this turn in the controversy, Jesus' enemies seek to arrest him; but they fail "because his time had not yet come." One group believes in Jesus because his signs correspond with those predicted for the messianic age (verse 31).

❏ *John 7:32-52.* On the last day of the festival, Jesus makes his central proclamation: "If anyone is thirsty, let him come to me and drink" (verse 37). He made the same promise to the Samaritan woman. Jesus' gospel is universal, a promise to all humankind and an invitation to all to share in the salvation he brings.

Jesus, however, speaks to a divided people where some have hatched schemes to do away with him. Ordered to arrest Jesus (verse 32), the Temple guards fail to carry out their assignment (verse 44). Their excuse for negligence: Jesus' words are unprecedented. "No one ever spoke the way this man does!" (verse 46). The Temple guards are awed by Jesus.

Jesus here speaks according to the symbolism of the Feast of Tabernacles. The service for this occasion reminds the Jews that water had been given from the desert rock to their ancestors when the people were famished. Each day the religious leaders fill a golden pitcher with water and, carrying the water, march to the Temple. On the last day of the feast, the people celebrate their coming to the land of promise, with its abundance of water, by leaving their pitcher behind. Into this symbolism Jesus comes, promising "living water." He will satisfy the people's spiritual thirsts.

Jesus will give the people inspiration and power to do the will of God. He proclaims himself as the source of living water. His words, John adds, refer to the mighty work of the Holy Spirit who is to come. The people, receiving the Spirit, will produce a nobler service to God than they have ever dreamed could be.

What do the people say when they hear Jesus' words? Some say he is the prophet promised of old. Others say he is the

Christ. Some question whether the Messiah is to come from Galilee. Don't the Scriptures say he will be a descendant of David who came from Bethlehem? Still the people are divided over him, but no one will lay hands on him.

The Pharisees are angered after the Temple guards fail to arrest Jesus. They rage: "You mean he has deceived you also?" (verse 47). No Pharisees will believe in Jesus. But the despised crowd, who do not know the law, are accursed. The crowd do not know the ancient ceremonial law. The Pharisees were contemptuous of the common people. When Nicodemus tried to introduce reason and fairness into the discussion, they scoffed at him. He was told to search the Scriptures. Then he would see that no prophet was to come out of Galilee.

❏ *John 7:53–8:11.* By refusing to condemn the woman taken in adultery, Jesus avoids the trap laid for him by the Pharisees. Jewish law commanded that this woman be stoned to death for her sin. If Jesus condemns her for her sin, he loses his reputation as a friend of sinners and loses the name for love and mercy he has earned. He will also break the Roman law, for Jews could not pass the death sentence on anyone. On the other hand, if Jesus says that she should be pardoned, he will break the Jewish law and be accused of encouraging adultery.

Instead, Jesus shows his compassion for the woman and turns the Pharisees' accusation back on them by saying, "If any one of you is without sin, let him be the first to throw a stone at her" (verse 7). When they all leave and no one is left to accuse her, Jesus tells the woman, "Neither do I condemn you. . . . Go now and leave your life of sin" (verse 11).

❏ *John 8:12-20.* The Court of the Women in the Temple is the scene of Jesus' proclamation. Here during the Feast of Tabernacles the people bring their money and drop it into thirteen treasure chests. This money was used to pay for the upkeep of the Temple, for buying the two doves a woman required for her purification after her child's birth, and for gifts to keep the altar fires lighted. The money dropped into the treasury also paid for the incense used in the Temple services. The Temple treasury was a place where a person or a family could give money to the treasure chests in thanksgiving for what God had done for them.

Many people trek to the Temple treasury. So it was an excellent place for teaching the devout. On the first day of the Feast of Tabernacles, the Jews held a service that they called the Illumination of the Temple. The service was held in the Court of the Women. To this court, with its large galleries, the spectators came. Here they were confronted by a great drama of light, for in the center of the court stood four huge candelabra. At the coming of darkness these candelabra were lighted so that they sent brilliant illumination, it was said, through the whole city of Jerusalem. Then the wise and holy priests of Israel danced and sang songs of praise.

❏ *John 8:21-59.* In this section Jesus challenges us to belief in him. Jesus bids us think about the true nature of discipleship. What does it involve?

William Barclay, in his commentary *The Gospel of John* (Revised Edition, Volume 2; The Westminster Press, 1975; pages 20–22), describes discipleship in four parts. (1) "Discipleship begins with belief." As soon as we accept Jesus' words as true, our discipleship begins. (2) "Discipleship means constantly remaining in the word of Jesus." We must listen to Jesus' words, learn from Jesus' words, penetrate the truth of Jesus' words. (3) "Discipleship issues in knowledge of the truth." The truth that Jesus teaches shows the real values of life. (4) "Discipleship results in freedom." Jesus' service brings freedom from fear, from self, from other people, and from sin.

DIMENSION THREE:
WHAT DOES THE BIBLE MEAN TO ME?

Jesus and Our Picture of Him

The enemies of Jesus presented a fantastic array of opinions concerning Jesus' character and mission, but it is our task to see for ourselves what he said and did. What is our picture of Jesus? A wild-eyed reformer? A weak, down-at-the-heels religious leader? Think of paintings you have seen of Jesus. Which ones pleased you? Which ones did you dislike? What does it matter to you that Jesus be presented as the Son of God? as a life-affirming, strong person?

Jesus' teaching led to divisions among the people. What signs do you see that his truth divides people today? What are the issues that divide church members?

What does it mean for you to come to Jesus and drink the living water? Give instances where his support has strengthened you for making decisions.

Consider the attitudes of church members you have seen in regard to dealing with wrongdoers. How would your church respond to a woman taken in adultery? What does it mean to hate the sin but love the sinner?

How is Jesus the light of the world? How has he been the light to you?

What does it matter whether we believe in Jesus? What does it mean for you to believe in him?

What does Jesus tell us about knowing the truth and the relationship of this knowing to freedom? What does this involve for you as a member of the church? What does it tell us about improving our minds?

"I am the good shepherd; I know my sheep
and my sheep know me . . .
and I lay down my life for the sheep" (10:14-15).

5

Jesus the Good Shepherd
John 9–10

DIMENSION ONE:
WHAT DOES THE BIBLE SAY?

Answer these questions by reading John 9

1. What do Jesus' disciples ask him about the "man blind from birth"? (9:2)

2. How does Jesus answer them? (9:3-5)

3. What does Jesus do next? (9:6-7a)

4. What happens to the man born blind? (9:7b)

5. What happens next? (9:13-16)

6. What do the Jews do? (9:18-29)

7. How does the man answer? (9:30-33)

8. How does Jesus answer all this? (9:35-38)

Answer these questions by reading John 10

9. What image does Jesus use to describe himself? (10:1-15)

10. What does Jesus say about other sheep? (10:16)

11. Jesus' words cause what reaction? (10:19-21)

12. What do the Jews ask Jesus in the Temple? What does Jesus reply? (10:22-30)

13. How do the Jews respond to Jesus? (10:31)

14. What does Jesus say to them, and what is their answer? (10:32-33)

15. How does Jesus answer their charge? (10:34-38)

16. What happens then? (10:39-42)

DIMENSION TWO: WHAT DOES THE BIBLE MEAN?

❏ *John 9:1-12.* This story plunges us into a basic discussion of the Old Testament belief that the sins of parents are visited on the children. Many Jews believed that an affliction like blindness was divine punishment for the sins of one's parents. They quoted the Scriptures: "I, the LORD your God, am a jealous God, punishing the children for the sin of the fathers to the third and the fourth generation" (Exodus 20:5b).

When Jesus is confronted by this Old Testament teaching, he does not try to unravel the theoretical relationship between sin and suffering. He replies that the man's affliction fell on him to reveal how God can work in human experience. Jesus' miracle with the man is a sign of the working of God's power. God's glory resides in the divine compassion. God's compassion in the healing is a manifestation of God's grace. It gives the afflicted one an opportunity to show what is happening to him or her. While calamity may strike the person who is unfaithful and demolish that person, the same calamity can serve to strengthen the individual who is faithful.

We see this fact proved daily. Recall when trouble was used to lift you to more noble existence.

What Christian has not felt that God graciously uses bitter experiences to bring out the best in people? A person may become more aware that God is using him or her to bless the life of others. A dread disease, for example, may strike two women. One woman falls victim to despair, while the other gives her final days to demonstrate the love of God to others who are afflicted with that disease.

Jesus now warns his followers that they must do the work of God while there is still time (9:4). God gives us time for work and time for rest, and Jesus says we must do the work of God while there is still time. Night will come when no one can work. Our purpose as Christians is to use the time we have for God's service. If we do not do this, darkness will overtake us. Jesus says, "While I am in the world, I am the light of the world" (9:5). Jesus means that the time for our relating ourselves to him is short. We have the time to respond to Jesus as our Savior or to miss this great opportunity.

Jesus' method of healing may strike us as being unhygienic and crude. But Jesus is being true to the Incarnation. In his use of saliva to make mud for healing, Jesus identifies himself with the life around him. Saliva and mud healings were used in his culture. Jesus knew that many Jews believed there is healing power in saliva and mud. He knew that the effectiveness of a physician's treatment depends to a great deal on the believer's faith. Jesus shared fully our human life.

❏ *John 9:13-23.* "Now the day on which Jesus had made the mud and opened the man's eyes was a Sabbath." Healing was a form of work, and Jewish law did not allow work on the sabbath. The Pharisees were up in arms over Jesus breaking the sabbath. They called the healed man to a hearing. Under questioning, the man told them simply what had happened. Some of the Pharisees said Jesus was not from God or he would not violate the sabbath. Other Pharisees disagreed. How could a man who was a sinner perform such signs? The Pharisees were divided. They asked the man his opinion. The man said, "He is a prophet." This response was bold for one who had spent his life begging.

The Jews disputed the reality of the cure. They summoned the man's parents for questioning. The parents testified that the man was their son. They said he had been born blind. Since their son was of age, the parents said, let him answer the Pharisees' questions. The parents did not want to be thrown out of the synagogue.

❑ *John 9:24-34.* The Pharisees angrily insult the man, but they still are up against his testimony: "I was blind but now I see!" This testimony the Pharisees cannot dispute. The man knows what has happened to him. Jesus has given him sight.

Jesus deals with the healed man on two levels. First is the level of pure miracle. The man receives physical sight. Second is the level of spiritual sight. The sign (miracle) points to a deeper reality. The sign is a parable of what may happen to us when we encounter the Christ. He saves us from blindness. He takes the dark away. He is the light of the world. Under Jesus' light our whole life is renewed.

❑ *John 9:35-41.* The man cast from the synagogue faces humiliation and disgrace. But the story is not over yet. Jesus knows what is going on. He knows that the man has been treated cruelly. Jesus goes out, finds the man, and reveals himself to the man. Jesus is the Son of Man, who calls for commitment. And the man's response? He replies, "Lord, I believe," and worships Jesus.

Jesus then challenges the man concerning the divine judgment. Jesus declares he has come into the world for judgment—that those who see might become blind. Surely they will say, "We are not blind." But God's judgment holds. The Pharisees are blind, else they would not continue in sin. They think they have full knowledge of the truth. If so, Jesus says, they should be held responsible. The more they know, the more will be expected of them.

❑ *John 10:1-21.* A basic principle in reaching the right solution in working acrostics and crossword puzzles is that we move from the known to the unknown. We make use of what we already know to discover what we have not known before. So it is with our understanding of the Bible and Christian faith. When John depicts Jesus as the good shepherd, he is using the known to uncover the unknown.

The Jews could look at the history of Israel and conclude: "The LORD is my shepherd, I shall not be in want" (Psalm 23:1). They could say: "You led your people like a flock / by the hand of Moses and Aaron" (Psalm 77:20). Turn to some of the other beautiful passages in which God is portrayed as a good shepherd, for example, Psalm 95:7; 100:3; Isaiah 40:11; and Ezekiel 34.

So, like a Palestinian shepherd, Jesus comes to us. The shepherd works in lowliness. He carries a sling to defend the sheep from wild animals. He uses a staff, or small wooden club, to ward off enemies—wild beasts and human robbers. He pulls the sheep back from danger with his crook.

The Palestinian shepherd is a gentle but powerful person in whom power takes second place to love. The sheep know his voice—a voice that calls them to safety. They respond to his voice, and he leads them out of danger to places where they can find pasture. They hear and understand his voice, and they are not pulled into the wrong course advocated by strangers.

Do we know his voice? How do we recognize Jesus' voice? These are questions that we face with feelings of urgency today. Sometimes religious groups make fantastic statements to the effect that they have heard the voice of Jesus. By their attitudes and activities they would have us believe that Jesus' voice is one of fanaticism and violence. They claim that they have Jesus' sanction for fanatical and selfish conduct. Christians, however, recognize Jesus' voice as a voice of calm and reason. It is the voice of humility, never of bitterness and bigotry. Christians are often asked to listen to strange voices. How do we distinguish Jesus' voice?

Once I was asked if I would answer hate telephone calls that were coming in from enraged people in a neighborhood beset by racial conflict. We wanted to find out if a spirit of calm reasonableness might lesson a mob psychology. So while special police officers patrolled the neighborhood, I answered the phone calls.

I spent a harrowing and wearying night trying to speak a healing and reconciling word to irate callers. Sometimes I had no chance to speak at all. The callers delivered insults and threats and then hung up the phone.

42

In some cases I was able to get a hearing. I told my hearers that I was a Christian minister who wanted to be a witness for Christ in the tense situation. At this point some callers said that they were Christians themselves and that Jesus supported them in their attitude. I tried to reason with them, and in some cases I succeeded. I asked them how they could engage in a hate campaign in the name of Jesus and whether they were listening to the voice of Jesus in this dangerous situation.

My question seemed to give the callers pause. Challenged to reason, they either ended the conversation at once or tried to involve me in arguments. But the burden of my response was on the need of us all to listen to the voice of the good shepherd.

❏ *John 10:22-42.* During the Festival of Lights or Festival of Dedication (the Jewish Hanukkah, which falls near our Christmas), Jesus makes his supreme claim. For us this is important, for it comes at a time when the Jews celebrated the victory of their people over the attempt of a Syrian army to wipe them out as a people (about 164 B.C.). The festival is a triumphal celebration that grew out of a dark time, just as our salvation came out of the most bitter of human experiences: Jesus' death on the cross.

Jesus chose this time of joyous celebration to announce who he is. The weather was "wintry" when he spoke. The Jews found him on Solomon's porch and demanded that he no longer keep them in suspense. He had told the Jews already that he was the Son of God, the light of the world, the bread and water of life. Confirming these claims, Jesus said, were his mighty works. In him God was speaking to all humankind, promising eternal life to those who accepted him.

Jesus' mighty works were bound up with Jesus' trust in God. Jesus' supreme claim depended on this reality in which he confronted the people: "I and the Father are one" (10:30). This statement was a statement, not of philosophy, but of relationship. Jesus' oneness with God was based in perfect love and perfect obedience. God was in Christ. God asks us to accept Jesus' deeds—to base our decision on what Jesus does.

DIMENSION THREE:
WHAT DOES THE BIBLE MEAN TO ME?

John 9 and 10—Guidance for Daily Life

Reflect on some themes in the Scripture passages for this lesson. Choose the themes that concern you most deeply and meditate on their meaning for you.

Why do you think Jesus used saliva to make mud to heal the man blind from birth? What does his action imply for Christians today?

What does it mean to you that the man said, " I was blind but now I see"? Have you ever had this experience?

Do you know persons who believe that physical afflictions are punishment for sins? How should we meet physical and emotional calamities? When have you seen the work of God manifested in troubles?

How do you spend your time? What changes should you make in your use of it?

How is the good shepherd portrayed in this lesson? How is Jesus your good shepherd?

"I am the resurrection and the life. He who believes in me will live, even though he dies; and whoever lives and believes in me will never die" (11:25-26).

—— 6 ——
The Resurrection and the Life
John 11–12

DIMENSION ONE:
WHAT DOES THE BIBLE SAY?

Answer these questions by reading John 11

1. What does Jesus say about the illness of Lazarus? (11:4)

2. What do the disciples say to Jesus when he says they must go back to Judea? (11:8)

3. What does Jesus say about Lazarus's death? (11:11, 14-15)

4. What do Martha and Mary do when Jesus arrives? (11:20)

5. When Jesus sees Mary weeping, what does he say? (11:33-34)

6. What does Jesus do next? (11:38-43)

7. What is the reaction of the crowd? (11:45-46)

8. What does Caiaphas, the high priest, tell the Sanhedrin? (11:49-52)

9. What happens as a result of the Sanhedrin's meeting? (11:53)

10. What happens next? (11:54-57)

Answer these questions by reading John 12

11. What do Jesus' friends do for him when he comes to Bethany? (12:2-3)

12. What is Judas's question about Mary's act? (12:4-5)

13. How does Jesus respond to Judas? (12:7-8)

14. What does the crowd do? (12:9)

15. What do the chief priests plan to do? (12:10-11)

16. What does the crowd do next? (12:12-13)

17. What does Jesus do then? (12:14-15)

18. What is Jesus' response to the questions of the Greeks? (12:23-26)

19. How do various ones, including Jesus, respond to the voice from heaven? (12:29-32)

20. Why do many not believe in Jesus despite his signs? (12:37-41)

21. Why do others not express a belief in Jesus? (12:42-43)

DIMENSION TWO:
WHAT DOES THE BIBLE MEAN?

❑ *John 11:1-16.* Everything in John's Gospel should be understood in the light of the Resurrection. The theme of resurrection may be seen in Jesus' discussions with Martha and in the raising of Lazarus from the dead (11:24-44). The sign that Jesus performed at Lazarus's tomb points to the mightiest of God's acts.

Martha and Mary are distressed over the sickness of their brother. They send a messenger to report their anxieties to Jesus. Their call is urgent, and they want Jesus to come at once to Bethany. But Jesus delays his coming for two days.

Why does Jesus delay? He sees the impending death of Lazarus from a different viewpoint. He is concerned that God's purpose in Lazarus's death be revealed. Martha and Mary are concerned with Lazarus's physical death. Jesus states that Lazarus's "sickness will not end in death. No, it is for God's glory." Also the Son of God may be glorified by it.

The story points to Jesus as the Lord and Conqueror of sin and death. So Lazarus's death is a link in the chain of events. Lazarus, Jesus says, has fallen asleep; and Jesus will go to awaken him. If he is sleeping, the disciples reply, Lazarus will recover. Then Jesus focuses on the deeper issue of death: Lazarus has indeed died. Jesus wants to show forth God's glory in this event. So he bids the disciples go with him to the tomb. Thomas, seeing the danger into which they will go, says, "Let us also go, that we may die with him."

Jesus and the disciples know that the Jews are ready to stone Jesus to death, but Jesus reminds the disciples of another reality: Jesus is the light of the world. Now the disciples walk in the light, and their walking in his light makes them secure against stumbling. Jesus knows the disciples need have no fear of going into Judea, for his hour has not yet come.

The forces of evil are gathering, but Jesus still has some time before his death. If the people will walk with him, they will be in the light.

Why return to Judea? Jesus begins to explain: Lazarus our friend has fallen asleep. The whole event of his death is meant to strengthen the disciples' faith, a faith that is still not secure. The disciples have faith, but in the final hour they will forsake him and flee. They have not yet faced the supreme test of discipleship.

❑ *John 11:17-37.* The friends of Jesus are in their time of bereavement when Jesus arrives in Bethany. More than three days have passed since Lazarus's death. When Martha knows Jesus is on his way, she goes out to meet him, leaving her sister Mary in the house. Martha says to Jesus: "Lord, . . . if you had been here, my brother would not have died." Martha makes no special petition to Jesus. She knows that whatever Jesus asks of God will be done. Jesus says to her simply, "Your brother will rise again." Martha knows that Lazarus will rise again at the resurrection on the last day, but she is not ready for the response Jesus makes in verses 25-26. Jesus is the final resurrection. He gives eternal life now. Fellowship with God is possible here and now. This fellowship comes to its full flowering in the triumph over death. Eternal life, life with an entirely new quality is possible now.

Martha makes her full confession. She commits herself to the Christ, the Son of God, the Messiah—the fulfillment of all human hopes.

❑ *John 11:38-44.* Jesus issues three brief directions at the tomb: "Take away the stone," "Lazarus, come out!" and "Take off the grave clothes and let him go." Let us consider the symbolism of these words.

Take away the stone. This direction may remind us of that stone of power that weighs life down. Our lives may be shut up in fear, worry, or hostility, so that these stones literally kill us. We need some power greater than ourselves to wake us from the death. The Resurrection is that power.

Lazarus, come out! Lazarus lies dead, unable to exercise his will. Yet by the grace of God even the dead may be spoken to. Lazarus is testimony to the reality that the purpose of religion is to wake us from the dead.

Take away the grave clothes and let him go. We may be held fast in grave clothes—old sorrows and anxieties, old sins and habits that imprison us daily. The Resurrection breaks these fetters. Lazarus is called from the grave. The dead man is raised to life;

the prisoner can now go free. He is loosed to the freedom of Christ and allowed to go home.

Home to what? Home to his true environment where by God's grace he lives in faith, hope, and love? Lazarus is sent back into ordinary life, but now there is a vast difference in his existence. Once Lazarus may have centered everything in himself, his goal being to manipulate others for his own advantage. But now Lazarus is called to be human—that is, to be responsible. He lives by a new commandment—to love one another. Who is Lazarus? He is each of us.

❑ *John 11:45-57.* Jesus' words and actions produce divisions among the people. Many Jews have seen his great sign of resurrection and have been shaken by his power over death. For some persons Jesus' mission prompts faith, while for others it drives them away to the Pharisees, giving the Pharisees more evidence against him.

The Sanhedrin is called together (11:47). The Sanhedrin was the official Jewish high court composed of seventy teachers of the law, over which the high priest presided. While the authorities are expressing their anxieties concerning the possible destruction of the Temple and the nation itself by the Romans, a strange prophecy emerges. Caiaphas, high priest for the year, accuses the Council members of knowing nothing at all. He predicts that one man will die for the whole nation.

From this time onward, the situation gets more tense. The Council determines to put Jesus to death, so he has to be wary of his movements. The chief priests and the Pharisees put out a notice that anyone who can find Jesus should let them know so that he can be arrested. All eyes turn toward Jerusalem at the Passover Feast where the final drama will be played out.

❑ *John 12:1-11.* Jesus' time has come. He is ready for that momentous period the church calls Holy Week.

Jesus goes to Bethany where Lazarus is and where Martha serves supper to him. His visit there is marked by Mary's unforgettable act—the anointing for his burial. Jesus is in grave danger. His foes have gathered the evidence against him and have condemned him to death.

Mary's self-giving act may be seen by an insensitive world as wasteful. Judas expresses what we have all felt at some time:

"Why wasn't this perfume sold and the money given to the poor? It was worth a year's wages."

Jesus refuses to encourage a conflict between Mary's devotion and the needs of the poor. The love that breaks the container of the precious ointment for anointing Jesus' body for burial would not neglect the needs of the poor. Mary has done what she can to bear witness to that love.

❑ *John 12:12-19.* As Jesus enters Jerusalem, he dramatically shows himself as the Messiah. He rides on a lowly colt, and the people shout "Hosanna!" and spread palm branches before him. (*Hosanna* was an expression directed to God. It meant "O save!" Later *Hosanna* became a cry of joyful acclamation.) Jesus comes in lowliness, reversing the standards of this world.

❑ *John 12:20-36a.* The rest of John's Gospel deals with the events of Jesus' persecution, trial, death, and resurrection. Jesus now faces the hour when he will be glorified on the cross.

Jesus' glorification is a strange glorification. Review and summarize the words of John 12:23-26. Anyone who hates the shoddiness of this wicked world will find true life. Anyone who serves Jesus must follow him.

Jesus first prays to God to be saved from this hour. Then Jesus remembers that for this hour he has come into the world. He hears a voice from heaven confirming the divine reassurance. Reality changes appearances. Jesus will go to the cross, and his going will be a judgment on the world.

❑ *John 12:36b-50.* Jesus withdraws from public view for a while. John finds the reason the people do not believe in Jesus in the message of the prophet Isaiah.

Isaiah too was rejected by a careless world. In these verses (Isaiah 53:1; 6:10) Isaiah is writing from a broken heart. He says that for all the good that was done through his words he may as well not have prophesied. Jesus must have felt somewhat the same. After all Jesus' acts and teachings, the people still do not understand his message.

In his last words spoken to the general public, Jesus makes one final plea that they recognize God in him. "When [a person] looks at me, he sees the one who sent me" (12:45). Jesus has come to bring enlightenment to God's people. Jesus brings the enlightenment of freedom from fear, freedom from ignorance, and freedom from sin.

God's love sent Jesus to be our Savior, not our Judge (12:47b). Anyone who hears Jesus' words and does not follow them is judged by these words. A person is not blamed for lack of knowledge; but if a person knows the path to follow and chooses another path, that person is condemned for his or her choice.

DIMENSION THREE:
WHAT DOES THE BIBLE MEAN TO ME?

John 11 and 12—Guidance for Daily Life

1. We say that the essential point in Christianity is the reality that Jesus Christ is God's spokesman and representative. Jesus demonstrates and makes plain that he is the self-utterance of God. What does Christ's coming mean for our lives?

2. To trust in Christ means to trust in God. We affirm that Christ and God are one. How does this affirmation affect our conduct?

3. Christ's purpose is to seek and to save the lost. How does Christ find us?

4. Jesus came, not to judge, but to save. His life and death reiterate this reality. What are times when, deserving the judgment of God, you experienced God's mercy?

5. "His command leads to eternal life." Christ's commandment points us, not to a rule book, but to eternal life. This commandment is given for our wholeness, the meaning we live by, peace, and purpose.

"Peace I leave with you; my peace I give you. . . . Do not let your hearts be troubled and do not be afraid" (14:27).

— 7 —

The Way and the Truth and the Life

John 13–14

DIMENSION ONE: WHAT DOES THE BIBLE SAY?

Answer these questions by reading John 13

1. What does Jesus know that gives him the power and the will to wash the disciples' feet? (13:3)

2. What does Jesus do before the Feast of the Passover? (13:4-5)

3. What does Simon Peter say when Jesus comes to him? (13:6-9)

4. How does Jesus answer Peter? (13:10)

5. What does Jesus say after he finishes the washing? (13:12-16)

6. What does Jesus say about his disciples? (13:17-20)

7. How is the betrayal of Judas Iscariot presented? (13:21-30)

8. What does Jesus say about the glorification of God and of himself? (13:31)

9. What counsel does Jesus give to his disciples? (13:33-35)

10. What does Simon Peter ask? (13:36a)

11. What is Jesus' reply? (13:36b)

12. What does Jesus say to Peter when the disciple vows to lay down his life for Jesus? (13:38)

Answer these questions by reading John 14

13. What assurance does Jesus give to the disciples? (14:1-21)

14. What additional assurances does Jesus promise? (14:25-31)

DIMENSION TWO:
WHAT DOES THE BIBLE MEAN?

❏ *John 13:1-20.* Have you ever been asked to do menial tasks that you thought were degrading and beneath your dignity? Did you feel bitterly resentful that you should be subjected to what you considered to be humiliation? If so, you can identify with the disciples who came to supper before the Passover. The task of washing the feet of weary travelers was usually performed by a servant or slave, but in poor homes it was performed by the family members. It was a simple task, a duty considered by some persons, including the disciples, as dirty work.

The disciples are in the midst of their meal when suddenly they realize something is amiss. They see Jesus rise from supper, lay aside his outer cloak, tie a towel around his waist, and begin to wash their feet.

Jesus' hour had come to leave the world. These verses tell us many things that Jesus knew. He knew that his hour for glorification had come, that his death was approaching. He knew that God had loved God's children to the end. He knew that the devil had already moved Judas Iscariot to betray him. Jesus also knew that God had given all power into his (Jesus') hands. Knowing that he had come from God and was going to God, Jesus understood his own origin and destiny.

In his actions here Jesus impels us to concentrate on the meaning of these acts for us. We do not know how to respond to love's demands because we do not know from whence we came or where we are going. We do not know who we are. When we know our origin—that we have come from the loving hand of God—we can rise to our full dignity as human beings. That means the most menial of tasks becomes a service of honor and love, a task in which we find our glory. When through Christ's grace we know that we are intended for eternity and will find our home in God, the little frettings and anxieties about ourselves come to an end.

So Jesus, facing the betrayal of Judas, gives us a lesson in humility, a lesson in how love responds to evil in the world. Judas's treachery hurt Jesus deeply. Jesus had chosen Judas to be one of his closest companions. How did Jesus respond to the hurt? He went on about his business of expressing God's love to God's children.

By his acts, Jesus was asking a question that the disciples had asked of him: "Who is greatest in the kingdom of God?" Was it persons who contended for the chief seats at huge public occasions? Those who strived to get prestigious positions of religious leadership? Those who insisted that they be Number One?

You come from God; you are going to God—therefore your status is secure. You do not need to strive after the fashion of lovers of this world. In the midst of the Last Supper, Jesus gives us an example of how we should treat one another. His example holds no spirit of competitiveness.

When Jesus comes to wash Simon Peter's feet, the disciple objects. Then Jesus tells him that if he does not wash Peter's feet, "You have no part with me." Peter replies, "Then Lord . . . not just my feet but my hands and my head as well!" Jesus, however, is suggesting more than an overall outer washing. He refers to the total and deeper cleansing of baptism and participation in his movement.

Would the disciples be great in the Kingdom? Mark 10:35-45 tells us Jesus' answer to that question. They would have to be baptized with the baptism with which Jesus has been baptized—the baptism of fire. Whoever would be great in the Kingdom "must be slave of all. For even the Son of Man did not come to be served, but to serve, and to give his life as a ransom for many" (Mark 10:44-45).

Luke 22:27c reports words characteristic of Jesus: "But I am among you as one who serves." That is the great and dramatic lesson of the events at the Last Supper.

These events deal also with the shame of Judas's disloyalty toward Jesus: "He who shares my bread has lifted up his heel against me" (John 13:18c). Jesus here uses a quotation from Psalm 41:9. In the Middle East to eat bread with someone meant one was friendly and loyal to a host. Persons felt peculiarly rejected, humiliated, and sorrowful when one who had eaten at their table was disloyal. The Hebrew phrase for this act of disloyalty emphasizes the bitterness that comes with such betrayal. It means the act is one of "brutal violence." In the fatal hour Judas committed this act.

❑ *John 13:21-30.* "Who, me?" That was the essential question of the disciples when Jesus told them one of them would betray them. They were perplexed. They looked at one another in puzzled ways. Jesus' words to them call each to ask of himself whether he is capable of the treachery. Christians today are bound to ask themselves the same question.

What has Judas done? Jesus probably asked Judas to sit in the place of honor on his left hand, according to Jewish custom. In the midst of the meal Jesus hands Judas the morsel, another symbol of special honor. Jesus is appealing to Judas not to carry out his plan for the betrayal. Not only would Judas be betraying his Lord but also he would be betraying himself.

Judas is ready to act now. Jesus, knowing the battle for Judas's soul has been lost, bids the disciple do his deed quickly. So Judas strengthens his resolve. When he has eaten the morsel, the devil enters into Judas; and he goes out to sell his Lord.

And it was night. A thousand sermons have been preached on these words, some of the most tragic words in human history. "It was night" because Judas, a man intended for a great destiny, had gone against divine love. Judas had decided to pursue his own ends. No longer would he participate in what he considered a lost cause. In the midst of an evil world, Judas rejected the light of the world—*and it was night.* Judas ended up lost and alone.

And it was night. The words are a parable of our human existence. How many times have we turned our backs on Jesus and decided to go our own way? *And it was night.*

THE WAY AND THE TRUTH AND THE LIFE **57**

❏ *John 13:31-38.* A strange thing happens. Judas goes out to do his deed, but Jesus does not denounce him. In God's reckoning the Son of Man has been glorified, an assertion of the power of God to bring good out of evil, light out of darkness. Judas's treachery becomes an instrument of God's providence. Jesus is glorified by the act that sends him to the cross. Jesus obeys God in the terrible chain of events, and in this way he glorifies God. Judas's betrayal becomes the means of expressing supremely the love of God to God's human children. The cross becomes the ultimate symbol of God's love to the human race.

Jesus turns to his farewell (John 13:33). Tenderly he says to his disciples that the time for him to be with them is short. They cannot go where he is going. He must go alone. But the One who will go the bitter way of Golgotha would have God's children honor God by obedience. The obedience is that "as I have loved you, so you must love one another." This direction was Jesus' farewell commandment. Love was at the center of God's redemptive purpose for our race—the center for each of us.

What is the secret of the divine glory? The secret is the sacrificial love of God, the love that heals, reconciles, redeems from evil, and sets us upon a new purpose in life. By our love the world will know we are Christ's disciples.

It is true. The world looks at Christians and the church and asks whether we walk in love.

❏ *John 14:1-14.* The powers of evil are gathering against Jesus and his small band of followers. Trouble is everywhere. Jesus' enemies are plotting to put him to death. His followers are no longer the huge crowds that once marveled at his wonderful deeds. They are a small band of dispirited and discouraged people who have seen already the terrors of the Roman handling of dissenters. Jesus' followers are raising questions about his meaning and purpose. Even trusted disciples are deserting him in disarray. Everything seems ready to collapse.

In the midst of social hostility and upheaval, Jesus speaks to his distressed disciples. They face trouble on every side, but he advises them to rise above trouble. How will this be done? "Trust in God; trust also in me." Put yourselves in the hands of everlasting mercy and courage. Though life should fall in, God's grace will not fail you. You are not without resting places in your journey. Jesus is going ahead of you to prepare many fine rooms for you. Believe what Jesus has told you about God.

So Jesus speaks to his first-century followers. So now he speaks to us: "Do not let your hearts be troubled." God's heaven has many abiding places that Jesus Christ has prepared for us. In a world where we often find no peace or security, Christ has come; and he will come again. He has prepared a place for us. He knows the way, for he is the way. "No one comes to the Father except through me." Would we find the way to God? It leads through Christ.

Jesus speaks to a world that thinks of God as a being who lives far off. Such a God is transcendent, and a gulf exists between this God and human beings. Jesus, in the experiences of the Last Supper, emphasizes that the gulf between the human and the divine is bridged.

Would we see God? Then let us look at Jesus. When we see Jesus, we see God—what God is like, what God values, how God acts toward his human children. Jesus comes to share fully in our human existence. He brings to us God's message of forgiveness and help.

Jesus brought the assurance to us that by God's grace we shall do even greater works than Jesus did. In this assurance Jesus demonstrates the divine humility.

❏ *John 14:15-24.* Life will be hard for you, Jesus says to his disciples and to us. You will face the entrenched evil of the world and the pains of sorrow and personal defeat. You will have to deal with sufferings and with rejection by the world. One thing you will not have to face—that is life without love, without God. In the most bitter of experiences God will be with you, bringing courage.

Jesus tells his disciples that life must be based in love; for God loves them. So if we love Jesus, we shall keep his commandments. Our love will be tested by our obedience. We are called to contemplate the supreme test of obedience that is seen in Jesus Christ, who has gone to the cross to achieve God's purpose for humankind.

Jesus demonstrates to his disciples that our love is tested daily. It is an act of love when one washes the feet of another—that is, when one exercises compassion and care for persons in their need, whatever it is. Sometimes we claim to prove our love for God, but we walk by the wounded on the other side of the road. Who are the wounded in our society? Street people? Those with handicaps? Victims of war, floods, and other natural disasters? Victims of economic exploitation? Victims of political oppression?

Make a list of the wounded in American society and in the world at large. What are Christians doing about these victims? How can you minister to them?

Jesus promises us that we shall face a hard existence if we want to show love to God, but he assures us we shall not fight our battle alone. He will send us a Helper, the Spirit of Truth, the Holy Spirit.

Who is the Holy Spirit? He is the *parakletos,* a Greek word meaning "helper," "counselor," or "comforter." *Parakletos* means a person who is called in, like a witness in a trial, a medical expert, or a special counselor. The Holy Spirit exercises the function of comforter and sympathizer in time of grief. Our word *comfort* is derived from the Latin *fortis,* meaning brave. So one who comes in times of trouble is one who comes to make us brave.

Jesus says the Holy Spirit will be given to us as counselor. The Spirit will guide us in the truth. The Spirit will come quietly and unobtrusively, like a dove descending on your lawn.

Jesus' point in all this is that he will never leave us alone. He will give us the Holy Spirit who will dwell with us forever.

❑ *John 14:25-31.* "The Counselor, the Holy Spirit," will teach us all things and will bring to our remembrance all that Jesus has said. The Spirit will give peace, but not as the world gives peace. The world, that part of creation estranged from God, deals in the "peace" of violence and conflict; but the peace of Jesus is something quite different. That peace is based in him who has repeatedly demonstrated he is "the way and the truth and the life."

DIMENSION THREE:
WHAT DOES THE BIBLE MEAN TO ME?

John 13:1-19—Jesus as Servant

We place a lot of meaning in our status in society. We would rather be among the leaders and be waited on than be a follower and have to wait on others. What example did Jesus give us for leading and serving? How can we enhance the quality of our living by being a servant?

John 13:21-30—Betrayal

How have you experienced a nighttime by being separated from God? What kinds of betrayal do you practice in daily life? by neglecting the needs of others?

John 14:1-7—"The Way and the Truth and the Life"

Jesus promised his disciples that where he was going they also could go. How do we find the way to go? What truth is Jesus teaching us in John 14:1-7? Have you found the life promised by Jesus?

John 14:27—"My peace I give to you"

Many groups today are calling for peace in our world. What is the difference between the peace they are seeking and the peace Christ gives us? How can the Holy Spirit help us find and keep this peace in our life?

*"In this world you will have trouble. But take heart!
I have overcome the world" (16:33).*

8

Jesus the True Vine
John 15–16

DIMENSION ONE:
WHAT DOES THE BIBLE SAY?

Answer these questions by reading John 15

1. What images does Jesus use to begin Chapter 15? (15:1-6)

2. What happens to the branch that bears no fruit? (15:2, 6b)

3. What happens to every branch that bears good fruit? (15:2)

4. What is the duty of the disciple? (15:4-7)

5. What happens if the disciple keeps Jesus' commands? (15:10)

6. Why has Jesus spoken to his disciples of these things? (15:11)

7. What is Jesus' command? (15:12)

8. When are the disciples called no longer servants but Jesus' friends? (15:14-15)

9. Why did Jesus choose the disciples? (15:16)

10. Why does the world hate the disciples? (15:18-19)

11. What will the Counselor do when he comes? (15:26)

Answer these questions by reading John 16

12. Why has Jesus told "all this"? (16:1)

13. What will happen to the disciples? (16:2)

14. Why will these frightful things be done to the disciples? (16:2b-3)

15. Where is Jesus going? (16:5)

16. What will be the role of the Holy Spirit? (16:8-15)

17. What does Jesus mean by the words "a little while"? (16:16-22)

18. What will Jesus' pledge of triumph do? (16:25-33)

DIMENSION TWO:
WHAT DOES THE BIBLE MEAN?

❑ *John 15:1-17.* Chapters 15 and 16 give us the longest mono-logue in John's Gospel. These chapters are from the farewell discourses of Jesus, and they contain only two short instances of conversation by the disciples. In 15:1-17, we have Jesus' theme of the mutual indwelling of himself and the disciples. This section and 15:18-27 set forth the pattern of the Christian's life.

The figure of the vine prevails until the allegory reaches verse 8. Jesus presents the idea of God as the one who plants and tills the world, humankind, and individuals. Jesus is the vine; God is the gardener/vinedresser; and the disciples are the branches.

The symbolism of the vineyard is from the Old Testament (see especially Isaiah 5:1-7) where the vineyard is the pople of God, planted by God and brought into nationhood by God. Psalm 80:8-15 recalls the history of Israel by describing the clearing of a vineyard, the bringing of a vine from Egypt, its transplanting, and its fine growth. But the vineyard falls into neglect and is left to suffer damage from trespassers and invading animals. Jeremiah 2:21 contains God's complaint that even though God planted a vine of good stock, the vine has degenerated.

Jesus talks with the disciples in pictures and ideas taken from the history of the Jewish people. Ezekiel 15 portrays Israel as the vine of God, and Hosea 10:1 declares, "Israel was a spreading vine." The vine was indeed the symbol of the nation of Israel.

"I am the true vine, and my Father is the gardener." Jesus is the fulfillment of God's redemptive activity with the Jewish people and the world. In Chapter 15, Jesus sets forth the character of the Christian life: *remain in me.* Jesus is the real or genuine Israel, realizing the calling in which the old Israel had failed. The church originates through union with Christ (verse 5), through prayer (verse 7), and through loving obedience (verses 9-10) that is expressed in joy (verse 11). The relationship of Christians to one another is love. Some readers of the Gospel have assumed that the love for one another applies only to the Christian fellowship, but John 3:16 would refute this narrow interpretation. Christians are called to love Christians, but we are also to love the world that God loves.

Isaiah and Jeremiah lamented that Israel, God's vineyard, had fallen to the ravages of the wild. Now Jesus proclaims that he is the true vine of God, and that Israel and the world should turn to him as the fulfillment of Israel's destiny.

The picture of the vine is intriguing. The grapevine grew lushly in Israel and, when it was properly tended, produced abundant yields of fruit. The vine grew rapidly, and careful pruning was necessary.

Some of the branches bear fruit; others do not. The useless branches have to be cut away. Their wood is only good for burning. Jesus tells his disciples that some of them are like the good branches of the vine. They bear abundant fruit because they abide in the vine (himself) and because God does the vinedressing. Other followers vowed to worship the Lord, but their lives proved they had turned away from the faith. They refused to listen to Jesus. Still others listened but refused to serve him. These followers were like wild vines whose uselessness caused them to be marked for burning.

"Remain in me, and I will remain in you. No branch can bear fruit by itself; it must remain in the vine. Neither can you bear fruit unless you remain in me." What does Jesus mean by these words?

Jesus bids us here to remember who we are and whose we are. He wants us to *remain* in his love—that is, to live in his love, to make it supreme, to endure without yielding up our faith, to bear patiently the trials that come to us as we make Jesus' love the most important concern of our lives. To abide in Christ means to share in his values. It means to keep in touch with the sources of our faith. We all know how important it is to keep in contact with these sources. We deplore the attitude of an airline pilot who fails to keep up with the latest technology. We do not like doctors who fail to keep up with the newest and best advances in their specialized fields.

When we abide in Jesus, we are in touch with the power that saves us from evil and turns our lives into joyous, vibrant avenues of service. When we are not abiding in him, we are like a useless wire detached from an electric circuit that gives power.

All this means that the Christian life must be a life of constant renewal through daily prayer and meditation, through study of the faith, and through associations with like-minded Christians. It means that we take the fellowship of the church seriously. We participate in its worship services, its learning opportunities, and its works of ministry. Abiding in Jesus means supporting the causes that Jesus would have us support—doing not just our wills but his.

Abiding in Jesus means living in love, what we might call a "chosen" existence. Jesus does the choosing.

We do not study all the options and finally out of our superior knowledge choose Jesus. He does the choosing of us. He chooses to call us friends instead of servants or slaves. He chooses to lay down his life for us and to give us a life of joy. He chooses to treat us as redeemed sinners, who may err but who by his grace may be forgiven and given a new start. He chooses to call us into a life of loving our fellow beings and the world that we all call home. Ours is a life of joy.

Jesus chooses each disciple to send us out. To send us out into what? He calls us to serve him in our daily occupations. He calls us to take risks in the world, for Jesus knows we cannot grow unless we understand that all life is hazardous. We grow through the testing of our powers.

Jesus sends us out to be his witnesses, to make disciples in his name. We are called to bear witness for him wherever we go, to convince persons around us by the quality of our living, not by our words.

As we have seen, Jesus chooses to answer our prayers. But these prayers must be in his name—that is, after Jesus' nature and will. With this standard for prayer, we shall not be able to pray for vengeance against enemies, for to do so means to usurp the prerogative of God. We shall be unable to pray for purely selfish things—things that would harm us or others. Unless we can say, "not my will, but yours be done," we cannot pray as Jesus tells us to pray.

❏ *John 15:18-27.* Jesus' words in John 15:1-17 were designed to impart peace and love to his followers, who were troubled about the changes and upheavals of their times. He wanted to inspire them with a message of joy in the hour of anxiety and fear. The disciples can face the worst; they can be of good cheer because Jesus has overcome the world. This joyful message is their great reason for confidence and hope in the future. Now Jesus' purpose is to warn the disciples of persecutions and sufferings to come.

Already the world's hatred of Jesus' followers is apparent. The world can tolerate people who practice its attitudes and values, but it inevitably hates those persons who reject its ways.

Jesus' faith repudiates the values of this world. Since the world hates him, it will hate his followers. He warns them to expect trouble. The world's hostility toward Jesus' followers is rooted in its ignorance and in its refusal to recognize that God is in Jesus' work. The world does not know him who has come from God.

The disciples could be consoled by the knowledge that the world's hatred of them clearly established the fact that they were supported by God. They were on God's side against the unbelief and hostility of the world.

John 15:26-27 tells us of the mission of the Counselor, the Holy Spirit. John 14:16 informs us that God will send the Counselor, while 16:7 says Jesus will send him. John unites the two seemingly contradictory ideas in the words "whom I will send to you from the Father" (15:26). The Counselor will bear witness to Jesus and to his followers because "you have been with me from the beginning." These witnesses have tested Jesus and have found him faithful and true.

❏ *John 16:1-22.* This section describes what will happen to the followers of Jesus in the persecutions. They will be driven from the synagogues—the worst disgrace that can come to any Jew. Their enemies will think that whoever kills them is serving God. The disciples' foes have not known God or Jesus.

Jesus reminds the disciples that none of them has asked where he is going. What he has just said to them has filled their hearts with sorrow and dread, but he assures them that it is to their advantage that he go away. If he should not go, the Counselor will not come; but if he goes, he will send the Counselor. It is necessary in God's redemptive purpose that Jesus be released from the barriers of physical existence and be available to the whole world. Jesus will now exert a new universal influence. He cannot be confined to the narrow bounds of Palestine.

Jesus must depart so the Holy Spirit can come. Jesus must leave the disciples so they can rise to their full possibilities as human beings. In other words, Jesus puts them on their own so that by the help of the Holy Spirit they may become more mature, more responsible.

"In a little while you will see me no more, and then after a little while you will see me" (16:16). Jesus describes the anguish of the disciples as like the anxieties and pains of a woman in labor giving birth to an infant. They will experience a season of sorrow, but sorrow will pass into joy. Here Jesus refers to the Resurrection, God's ultimate word to the human race. Jesus will win the final victory and bring to realization his kingdom on the earth. It will be a triumph that "no one will take away."

❏ *John 16:22-33.* Jesus here is offering comforting words to his disciples. The Jews believed in this present age and in an age to come. Between the two ages a time of judgment, the day of the Lord, would occur. This between-time would be a time of shattering all that is known to prepare for the new age.

Jesus uses these images to prepare the disciples for the suffering they will have to face. Beyond their suffering, however, Jesus tells them of the joy to come. This joy will be different from the world's joy—as Jesus' peace is different from the world's peace—in that this joy cannot be taken away and it will be complete, nothing will be lacking.

As the Christian's joy will be complete, so will our knowledge. Our questions will be answered fully. We will be in a new relationship with God—we can ask God for anything. We will understand, even as we are understood.

In these verses Jesus speaks plainly, not in figures. Jesus has come to earth from God and is now returning to God. Now Jesus' followers will have direct access to God—through Jesus. His death on the cross will open the way for humans to know that God is love.

Jesus' final words in this chapter illustrate his foresight and his knowledge of his followers. He predicts that the disciples will leave him—yet he will not be alone. God is with him.

Jesus is not holding the disciples' defection against them. He can love the disciples, and us, even though he knows that we are all weak. His love is realistic and sympathetic. Though he knows that he will be suffering greatly, Jesus' love enables him to love his disciples enough to prepare them for their suffering. Jesus reminds the disciples that his victory can be theirs too. "But take heart! I have overcome the world" (John 16:33).

JESUS THE TRUE VINE   **69**

DIMENSION THREE:
WHAT DOES THE BIBLE MEAN TO ME?

How does it make you feel as a Christian to be described as a branch on Jesus' vine? Is it comforting? Is it restricting? How can you know if your branch is being fruitful or being barren?

What kind of persecution have you felt because of being a Christian? In our country we do not face the martyrdom or extreme persecutions that first-century followers of Jesus felt. How, then, can these words warning of persecutions to come have meaning for us?

How has the Holy Spirit been your counselor? Jesus' death, horrible though it was, released the Holy Spirit into the world and released Jesus the Christ to a universal position where he is available to everyone. How is Jesus' victory in the Resurrection our victory in living?

"My prayer is not that you take them out of the world but that you protect them from the evil one " (17:15).

—— **9** ——

Jesus' Prayer of Adoration and Thanksgiving

John 17

DIMENSION ONE:
WHAT DOES THE BIBLE SAY?

Answer these questions by reading John 17

1. What does Jesus do before the disciples leave the upper room? (17:1)

2. What is Jesus' first petition? (17:1)

3. Of what does glorification of the Father consist? (17:2)

4. Of what does eternal life consist? (17:3)

5. How has Jesus glorified God on earth? (17:4-6)

6. Why does Jesus pray for the disciples? (17:9-11a)

7. What is Jesus' prayer to God on behalf of the disciples? (17:11b)

8. What has Jesus given the disciples? (17:14a)

9. Why has the world hated the disciples? (17:14b)

10. What more does Jesus pray for? (17:15-17)

11. For whom does Jesus now pray? (17:20-23)

12. How does Chapter 17 close? (17:25-26)

DIMENSION TWO: WHAT DOES THE BIBLE MEAN?

❑ *John 17: The High Priestly Prayer.* Jesus sums up his ministry in this chapter. Jesus here takes his place as the high priest did in the Jewish religion. The priest would enter the holiest place of the Jewish Temple to offer the blood of the slain sacrifice. As high priest for us here Jesus enters into God's presence and offers up his consecrated life for the sins of the world. Then he consecrates his disciples to his mission that they may be offered up in sacrifice—in obedience to God for the purpose of bringing the world to God. The prayer comes to us in three parts: Jesus prays for himself (verses 1-5), for his disciples (verses 6-19), and for the universal church (verses 20-26).

Chapter 17 is devoted solely to this final prayer of Jesus. It repeats much that has been said in the foregoing chapters of the Gospel. The prayer looks at the total picture of Jesus Christ and his work. Verses 6-8 give us a brief review of Jesus' ministry and what it has accomplished. They tell us that Jesus has made known God's name and nature to the disciples and glorified God on earth. The disciples have received the message of God's revelation and gained faith and knowledge as a result.

The main part of the prayer (17:6-19) deals with the disciples in their life in the world following Jesus' death. Jesus prays that his disciples may be kept in God's name (verse 11b), defended from the onslaughts of evil (verse 15), and sanctified in the truth (verse 19) so that they shall be one (verse 11b) and have Jesus' joy fulfilled in them (verse 13).

In verses 20-26, Jesus prays for all future believers, that they may be placed in the perfect unity of divine life shared by God and Jesus. In this way Jesus will be shown to the world, and his followers will be united with him.

❏ *John 17:1-5.* "The time has come." For what? The time has come for Jesus to be glorified in death. It will be a glorifying in triumph, since God has given Jesus sovereignty "over all mankind, to give eternal life to all whom [God] has given him" (*The Revised English Bible*). Jesus made known the goodness of God. He has manifested to the disciples the divine name God has given him. Jesus has accomplished the work that God has sent him to do. Now he is going to the cross for the sins of the world.

The cross is Jesus' glory? How?

By dying Jesus realizes his glory. His death is a summary of all he has stood for in the world. It reveals the very heart of

God—compassionate, emotional love giving itself to defeat evil and bring new life to the world. Jesus' death brings out the grandeur of the redemptive purpose of God. Jesus is *lifted up*, and his sacrifice tells us in an unmistakable way what God is like and what God's intention for us is. In the upper room we hear Jesus' words: "This is my body, which is for you." And we see and understand when we hear him say, "This cup is the new covenant in my blood" (1 Corinthians 11:24-25).

The cross completes Jesus' work on earth. It tells us what God's love is like, for God's love sacrifices to the limit. The cross is the supreme demonstration of God's love and care.

Another aspect of Jesus' final prayer is his petition that God would glorify Jesus and glorify God. We shall see that God answered this prayer by raising Jesus from the dead. In the Resurrection Jesus is victorious over sin and death.

The cross, then, was for Jesus the way back to God, his homecoming. Jesus had come from God; by his death he returned to God. Through the cross—"obedience unto death"—Jesus attained eternal life for all those whom God had given him. Eternal life means that Jesus imparts the very life of God to his disciples. They share in fellowship with God. They share the triumph and the joy of the Resurrection.

❏ *John 17:6-19.* Jesus begins this section with the assertion that the name, the very nature of God, has been manifested to the disciples: "I have revealed you" ("I have made your name known," New Revised Standard Version [NRSV]; verse 6). He has disclosed the divine nature to the ones God has given him. He has revealed this nature in signs and wonders, his mighty works, but also in his total life.

"They were yours; you gave them to me and they have obeyed your word" (verse 6). The disciples had not only heard the words of God and seen God's mighty works, they had heard God's call in Jesus and had been obedient, believing in Jesus' name. In accepting the teachings of Jesus the disciples had accepted the words of God. They had understood that Jesus came from God. Jesus' life among them was one great affirmation of the eternal God.

"I pray for them" (verse 9). Jesus is remembering that the disciples and we are set in a world hostile to the gospel. He prays that his disciples may be kept in God's mercy and tender care as they face the future.

"I am not praying for the world" (verse 9). The world includes the whole of creation and our human nature. Jesus came in love to redeem it from evil (3:16), and he has already overcome it (16:33). Jesus' prayer is a particular one. The faith of the disciples will finally win the world to Christ. The world cannot be penetrated by the gospel until the disciples are all one. So Jesus does not pray directly for the world here but for the disciples, who, after all, are part of the world (verse 15).

"I will remain in the world no longer" (verse 11). Jesus has come to earth and been active in it. He has shared fully in our human life. Now he faces death. He must leave the disciples, but they must remain in the world, with all its hostility. Jesus prays that God will watch over them according to the divine nature, that they may be one, just as God and Jesus are one. Jesus knows that a church disunited cannot represent the gospel to a world in desperate need. His petition is that God will join the disciples in strong unity of purpose, will, and dedication.

"I protected them" (verse 12). Jesus defended his disciples from evil; but one of them, Judas Iscariot, was destroyed "so that Scripture would be fulfilled." Judas was proof that the divine purpose could not be defeated. God used even Judas's treachery to carry out the divine will for the world.

"I have given them your word" (verse 14). These words repeat the thought of verse 8. They indicate Jesus' decisive help for his disciples. He has brought to them the word of God, a personal message disclosing the very nature of God to them. But because they are what they are, the world hates the disciples. They are not of the world, as Jesus is not of the world.

"My prayer is not that you take them out of the world" (verse 15). Jesus wants the disciples to remain in the world as his witnesses. They will obey another Master, not the evil one. They must stay in the world to advocate Jesus' sovereignty. We should remember that Jesus is sovereign—the ultimate strings of power are in his hands, but he will not exercise a "government in exile." He will rule human hearts from the cross. He will be mixed up in our human affairs, and he will send us into the human scene to be his witnesses. We are not allowed a "pie-in-the-sky" religion that retires from the pain and risk of life in society.

"But that you protect them from the evil one" (verse 15). The disciples will not be allowed an easy life that is protected from temptation, but they can be guarded from becoming enslaved by evil's corruption and power. Nowhere in John's Gospel does Jesus promise his followers they will be free of trouble and hardship. Jesus promises victory and joy.

"Sanctify them. . . . As you sent me into the world, I have sent them into the world" (verses 17-18). To be sanctified or consecrated means to be set aside for a sacred task. The church consecrates social workers, medical missionaries, educators, settlement house workers, diaconal ministers, bishops, and many others. As consecrated workers, these persons are witnesses for the gospel. Jesus consecrated his disciples in the truth. They were called to witness to the truth. Jesus equips the consecrated with the skills and refinements they will need to serve his cause in the world. Theirs will be a special responsibility—partnership with Jesus in the redemption of the world.

❏ *John 17:20-26.* Jesus' prayer in Chapter 17 begins with prayer for himself as he faces the cross. Then Jesus' concern widens— he prays for his disciples, that they may be kept safe and their faith remain strong. Now Jesus looks beyond the present to those who will follow him in the years and centuries to come.

Jesus prays for the unity of the church to come, "that they may be one as we are one: I in them and you in me" (verses 22-23). Jesus knew the strength that comes from unity in God's purpose.

In his last words to his disciples, Jesus' prayer speaks of glory—"I have given them the glory that you gave me" (verse 22). The disciples will find it difficult to see glory in the pain and suffering of Jesus' last hours or in their fear and uncertainty of the next weeks. But Jesus reminds them that the glory is theirs beyond the suffering.

DIMENSION THREE:
WHAT THE BIBLE MEANS TO ME

A Meditation

In his prayer for the universal church (John 17:20-26), Jesus confronts us with his concern for the redemption of the whole world. He knows that a divided and self-centered person will make for a divided church, a church that seeks to promote escapist religion.

In his prayer Jesus prays for us. Jesus exists in God's eternal love, and he wants us to exist in his love and the love of God. May we abide in Christ and may he abide in us that we may experience the oneness, the faith, hope, and love, that brings into being the universal church.

Jesus, the mediator of God's love, would make us captives of a world vision. He knows that nearness to God will draw us into a nearness to others, and he comes to make clear that we are not to despise others or the creation God has given to humankind. Jesus knows that we are sometimes indifferent to others, remote from them, unmoved by their cares and sufferings, though we may rub shoulders with them in the hurry and pressure of the common day. He knows that, left to ourselves, we may be heedless of the needs of others, deaf to God's call to us on their behalf, blind to the signs of God's mighty works in the world.

So Jesus prays for us as he did for the disciples long ago: "that they may be one." His is a prayer uttered out of love for us, for the universal church, and for the world. Jesus prays for us that in us all bitterness and strife may cease, that we may love and glory in the unity of the church; for unity is of God, and God's purpose for the universal church is to make it the means of world salvation.

So Jesus prays that as God has sent him into the world, the risen Christ may send us into the world to bear witness daily to God's renewal of life. Jesus' vision of a world redeemed rebukes us when we forget his compassion for all people and engage in practices that divide his church and weaken its witness.

So Jesus would move us from preoccupation with the big "I" to the gracious "we" that affirms the unity of his people around the world.

What are some ways you can work toward the redemption of the world? Does the world begin next door? Are there people in your community who need to receive God's love and to learn about Jesus' glory?

How does Jesus' prayer make you feel? Can you discover a personal message for you in the prayer?

"You are right in saying I am a king. In fact, for this reason I was born, and for this I came into the world, to testify to the truth" (18:37).

—— 10 ——
Jesus Is Arrested
John 18

DIMENSION ONE:
WHAT DOES THE BIBLE SAY?

Answer these questions by reading John 18

1. Where does Jesus go after he finishes the conversation with the disciples? (18:1)

2. What does Judas do? (18:2-3)

3. How does Jesus respond to the coming of this detachment? (18:4)

4. What happens then? (18:5-8)

5. What does Simon Peter do? (18:10)

6. How does Jesus react to Peter's action? (18:11)

7. What happens then? (18:12-14)

8. What does Simon Peter do now? (18:15-16a)

9. What does the girl on duty at the door say? (18:17)

10. What does the high priest do? (18:19)

11. What does Jesus tell him? (18:20-21)

12. What does one of the officials do after Jesus replies to the high priest? (18:22)

13. What does Annas do now? (18:24)

14. What happens to Peter, and how does he respond? (18:25-27)

15. Where do the soldiers and officials now take Jesus? (18:28)

16. What does Pilate do and say? (18:29)

17. How do they answer Pilate? (18:30)

18. What is Pilate's response? (18:31a)

19. What do the Jews say to this? (18:31b)

20. What now happens between Jesus and Pilate? (18:33-38a)

21. What does Pilate now tell the Jews? (18:38b-39)

22. What do the Jews say to this? (18:40)

DIMENSION TWO:
WHAT DOES THE BIBLE MEAN?

❏ *John 18:1-11.* Jesus finishes talking with his disciples. Afterward, he "left with his disciples and crossed the Kidron Valley. On the other side there was an olive grove, and he and his disciples went into it." The group often met here in the garden of Gethsemane. The term "Kidron Valley" was appropriate to the situation Jesus faced; for the name comes from a Hebrew word that means "to be dark" and "gloomy."

Judas, who was betraying Jesus, knew the garden well; for he had often gone there with Jesus. Bribed by the high priest's agents, Judas came there with a detachment of soldiers and some officers of the Pharisees. They brought lanterns, torches, and weapons. Consisting of Temple guards and a detachment of auxiliary Roman soldiers, the company that came to search for Jesus may have numbered several hundred men. Scholars have commented often on the size of the group that came to arrest Jesus, but Jesus' enemies were taking no chances. The authorities were suspicious of him; they feared his influence with the people, and they dreaded more turmoil. Also the Jewish authorities wanted to keep peace with the Romans. As for the Romans, they wanted order in the Jewish province they governed for the Empire.

The troops did not need to search for Jesus. He was not a refugee in hiding. When they appeared, Jesus, knowing what was going to happen to him, came forward and asked, "Who is it you want?" Not recognizing him, they said, "Jesus of Nazareth." The armed force was so astonished at Jesus' calm and dignity as he answered, "I am he," that its members were taken aback. They recoiled, some of them falling to the ground. Jesus repeated his question, and the crowd repeated the same response. John's Gospel does not contain the words of Mark: "Am I leading a rebellion . . . that you have come out with swords and clubs to capture me? Every day I was with you, teaching in the temple courts, and you did not arrest me" (Mark 14:48-49). Nor did John include Luke's scornful comment: "But this is your hour—when darkness reigns" (Luke 22:53). Jesus' calm manner, John's account convinces us, had the same effect on the searchers as did Jesus' comments recorded in Mark and Luke. The scene was highly dramatic.

Jesus' concern is now for his disciples. He says, "I told you that I am he. . . . If you are looking for me, then let these men go." Jesus is being apprehended because his enemies are charging him with high treason. It was dangerous for anyone to claim loyalty to Jesus. So Jesus is the good shepherd to his disciples, protecting them from harm. He has not lost a single individual whom God has given him. He does not want to risk the disciples' lives by associating them with himself at this point.

Jesus knows also that his whole movement could be wiped out if his precious corps of disciples should be killed. So nine men go their way, while Simon Peter and another disciple follow Jesus and the arresting company. Peter, however, proves his loyalty. It is proof in the wrong way—bad means to a good end. How many of us modern Christians follow Peter's example? To be sure, we do not seize weapons and strike out blindly at Jesus' enemies; but at times we may find ourselves acquiescing in measures of violence and cunning to prove our loyalty to God and country.

Simon Peter exercises courage and foolhardiness by drawing his sword and striking out at one of the band. He cuts off the ear, not of a soldier, but of the slave of the high priest. Peter has sworn his loyalty to Jesus, and he seeks to prove that loyalty. But Peter is very nervous, blustery as always, and quick to act on impulse.

What is Jesus' response? He calmly tells Peter, "Put your sword away! Shall I not drink the cup the Father has given me?" Did Shakespeare have this sentence in mind when he had Othello say, "Keep up your bright swords, for the dew will rust them"? This counsel is the admission that swords are useless in the situation faced by Shakespeare's characters.

❑ *John 18:12-27.* Events move fast in Jerusalem after Jesus' arrest. The Fourth Gospel, along with the other three, tells us that, following his arrest, Jesus was taken before the high priest for a trial. It was to be a preliminary hearing. Interwoven into the story of the ecclesiastical trials are the stories of Peter's denial.

Annas and Caiaphas were both high priests (Luke 3:2). Caiaphas, Annas's son-in-law, was serving in the office of high priest when Jesus was seized and taken before him. Caiaphas was president of the powerful Sanhedrin before whom Jesus would be brought to trial. Caiaphas had counseled the Jews that it was "better for you that one man die for the people" (John 11:50).

The detachment of soldiers, with their commander and officers, seized Jesus and bound him. Then they took him to Annas for the first hearing.

Meanwhile, Simon Peter and another disciple, who many interpreters have thought was John the beloved disciple, followed the armed company. This other disciple knew the high priest, so he spoke to the maid who was doorkeeper and brought Peter inside the courtyard where the servants and officers were standing and warming themselves. The other disciple thus used his influence to get Peter into the scene of the trial. The officers and men, their help no longer needed, had left Jesus in the hands of the Temple guards.

The other disciple apparently convinced the doorkeeper that Peter's intentions were right. Nevertheless, she asked Peter if he was a disciple of Jesus. Peter said he was not.

Annas questioned Jesus concerning his disciples and his teachings. Jesus replied that he had spoken openly to the world, having taught in the synagogues and in the Temple. He said he had done nothing secretly. Why did Annas question him? He should ask the people who had heard Jesus. This response drew the ire of an officer standing by, so that he was prompted to strike Jesus with his hand. Jesus replied that if he had spoken wrongly, the officer should have borne witness to the wrong; but if he had spoken rightly, why did the officer strike him? Jesus met the officer's violent act in a calm manner.

Annas then sent Jesus, bound, to Caiaphas. At this point, Peter was challenged again. He was standing in the courtyard warning himself at the fire when he was asked, "You are not one of his disciples, are you?" With this, Peter denied Jesus a second time. When a relative of the man whose ear Peter had cut off accused Peter of being a disciple of Jesus, Peter denied his Lord a third time. Immediately the rooster crowed, reminding Peter of Jesus' prediction that Peter would deny him three times (John 13:37-38).

❏ *John 18:28-38a.* Shortly after three o'clock in the morning, Jesus' captors took him from the court of the Sanhedrin to the praetorium, the governor's residence. The company of the

Jewish leaders did not go into the governor's palace because the Jews thought they would be defiled if they did. It was contrary to their religion to enter a pagan ruler's house. So Pilate met them outside.

Pilate came quickly to the point: What was the charge against Jesus? Pilate may have suspected a charge of treason against the Roman rule, but he needed to know the situation before sentencing the prisoner. He had to make sure the law of Rome was respected in the proceedings. He did not want to be used as a rubber stamp for the high priest's decisions. Roman law allowed no local authority to pronounce the death penalty. This grave responsibility was assigned to the governor as imperial Rome's representative.

The enemies of Jesus were demanding his death. Pilate cynically told them to judge Jesus by their own law, knowing that they could not do that. The Jewish authorities knew their limitations. They were not permitted to issue a decree of death. Verse 32 refers to the idea that Jesus "must be lifted up," meaning that he would die the death prescribed by Rome: crucifixion. The Jewish method of execution was by stoning.

What charge did the Jewish authorities level against Jesus? They brought a general accusation that Jesus was a criminal. Pilate knew that they meant more than that. Jesus was being accused of sedition, with claiming to be the king of the Jews.

Pilate threw aside the notion of calling his court into session. He interrogated the prisoner directly: "Are you the king of the Jews?" Then Jesus questioned Pilate: Is your question your own, or are you depending on what others have told you? Pilate replies that Jesus' own nation has delivered him into the governor's hands. Pilate says he is no Jew. He is not concerned with Jewish disputes. Pilate is contemptuous of the Jews. This prisoner before him looks like neither a king nor a revolutionary. What is his offense?

Jesus' offense? He says he is the Son of God, the Messiah (19:7). So he is claiming to be king of Israel.

Jesus is indeed king, but in a different sense than Pilate or the Jews imagine. His kingdom is not of this world. He rules, not by material might, but by love and compassion. He was born to be king—that is, to bear witness to the truth about God and God's will for human life. The kingdoms of this world are built on falsehood and violence, while Jesus' kingdom is built on love and right relationships with God and others. Jesus' kingdom is built on truth. His kingdom *is* truth. Pilate faces this reality with his question, "What is truth?"

Pilate was a cynical ruler charged with upholding the authority of the state. He was not equipped to deal with the nature of truth. He was impatient and wanted a resolution of one issue: What shall I do with Jesus of Nazareth? This is a question that concerns us all.

❏ *John 18:38b-40.* So Pilate failed to get his answer. He could not conceive of a lowly prophet in Jesus' position responding to this question with the astonishing claim, "I am the truth."

Pilate found no fault in Jesus, so he sought what he saw as an easy answer. He would put the decision back on the accusers. He would satisfy their anger and thirst for blood. Pilate put forward the choice—Jesus or Barabbas? As may have been expected, the crowd chose Barabbas, an insurrectionist and murderer (Luke 23:25). The crowd chose the Prince of Glory to be numbered with the transgressors.

DIMENSION THREE:
WHAT DOES THE BIBLE MEAN TO ME?

Reflections on the Scripture

A speaker for a program in a mental health institution was cautioned that her words might upset the patients. She quickly said, "Oh, let's not trouble ourselves about that. The patients will think I am talking about somebody else and will apply my words to somebody else—not to themselves."

Unfortunately, many Christians are like these patients when they read stories from the Bible. We need to be reminded often that the Bible is not just talking about Simon Peter, Pilate, and others. It is talking about us. We have said the Bible is a mirror in which we see ourselves. In the perplexities, misjudgments, sins, triumphs, and joys of its characters, we may see ourselves.

John's Gospel mirrors these realities for us in its stories of Simon Peter. In Chapter 18, Peter is shown as he is at the time;

but when we look beneath the surface, we get glimpses of what Christ would make of Peter. God did not call Peter to be anyone other than himself, his best self. So God also calls us to be our real selves, not to be imitations of the world around us.

This call means that Peter and we are being continually challenged to turn around from present attitudes and values, to grow, and to become our true selves. We all know how it is to hear a person who has not seen us in a long time say, "You haven't changed a bit!" Taken literally, those words mean that we have not grown; for we must change if we are to grow.

How do you change your attitudes and values? Reflect on the last five years of your life. What changes can you identify that you have made in your attitudes and values in these years? Can you pinpoint persons or incidents that brought about these changes? Do you like the attitudes and values you hold now? How can you use Jesus' words to effect changes you want to make in your attitudes and values?

JESUS IS ARRESTED

When he had received the drink, Jesus said, "It is finished."
With that, he bowed his head and gave up his spirit (19:30).

— 11 —
Christ Crucified:
"It Is Finished"
John 19

DIMENSION ONE:
WHAT DOES THE BIBLE SAY?

Answer these questions by reading John 19

1. What does Pilate do after the crowd cries out, "No, not him! Give us Barabbas!"? (19:1)

2. How do the soldiers treat Jesus? (19:2-3)

3. What happens then? (19:4-6)

4. How do the Jews respond to this? (19:7)

5. What is Pilate's response to this charge, and what does he do and say? (19:8-9a)

6. How does Jesus answer Pilate? (19:9b)

7. What does Pilate now say, and what does Jesus reply? (19:10-11)

8. What does Pilate seek to do then, and what do the Jews say to this? (19:12)

9. What does Pilate do when he hears these words? (19:13-14)

10. What do the Jews say to this? (19:15)

11. What does Pilate do then? (19:16)

12. Where do the soldiers take Jesus for crucifixion? (19:17)

13. When they crucify Jesus, what does Pilate write for a title to be put on the cross? How do the Jews respond to the title? (19:19-21)

14. What do the soldiers do that fulfills the Scripture? (19:23-24)

15. What does Jesus say from the cross to his mother and to the beloved disciple? (19:25-27)

16. What are Jesus' next words from the cross, and what do the soldiers give him? (19:28-30)

17. Who asks Pilate for the body of Jesus for burial? (19:38)

18. How does Nicodemus figure in the burial of Jesus? (19:39)

19. When and where is Jesus buried? (19:41-42)

DIMENSION TWO:
WHAT DOES THE BIBLE MEAN?

❑ *John 19:1-16.* Not Jesus but Pilate is on trial in John's account of Jesus' passion and death. Pilate is on trial before history and history's God. This is why Pilate nervously rushes about seeking some solution to the question: What shall I do with Jesus of Nazareth?

Pilate thinks he might have a way out of his dilemma by passing the responsibility for Jesus' acquittal or condemnation on to the crowd. He is foiled by the crowd's intense hatred. The fury of the mob tells Pilate he must placate the people. He well knows that the Jews can complain to Rome and get him fired from his post.

Pilate tries another tactic. He appeals to the emotions of the crowd. He takes Jesus and flogs him—that is, he has Jesus brutally whipped. When the Romans flogged a man, they bound him to a whipping post, so that his back was completely exposed. The soldiers used a leather thong last that was studded with pieces of lead and sharp bits of bone. The ordeal rendered most victims unconscious. Many went mad from the punishment. So Pilate thinks this punishment will satisfy the sadistic feelings of the mob. The people, he thinks, will see the lashing and will pity Jesus. Then Pilate can let the prisoner go.

Pilate, who did not want Jesus' blood on his hands, also thought that mockery of Jesus would be enough to soften the crowd's fury. The soldiers wove a crown of thorns and put it on Jesus' head. They dressed Jesus in a purple robe (a symbol of royalty). Then they hailed him as the king of the Jews and struck him with their hands.

Then Pilate brought Jesus before the crowd. Jesus, wounded from the beating, was wearing the purple robe and the crown of thorns. Pilate, showing Jesus to the crowd, deemed Jesus a pathetic figure. What a man to present himself as a king! Pilate said to the people: "Here is the man!" (19:5). But when the chief priests and officers saw Jesus, they were more insistent than ever that he be crucified. Jesus had threatened their whole way of life, and he had to be destroyed. Pilate said he found no crime in Jesus and told the Jewish authorities to take

CHRIST CRUCIFIED: "IT IS FINISHED" **91**

Jesus and to punish him by their own law. The Jewish leaders retorted that they had a law, and by that law Jesus ought to die. They knew that the death penalty was reserved to the Roman rulers. Jesus had committed the unforgivable sin of claiming to be the Son of God. At this Pilate became more afraid. He then asked Jesus, "Where do you come from?" Jesus may have been wearied from the cruel ordeal of his flogging and the ordinariness of the question, so he kept his silence. Pilate reminded Jesus that Pilate had power to free him or to destroy him. Jesus replied that Pilate's power was given to him by God to whom Pilate was finally responsible. Jesus was warning that Pilate was abusing his power.

Pilate again sought to release Jesus, but the Jews said Pilate was no friend of Caesar if he released Jesus. In other words, it would be unpatriotic and a violation of the duties of a Roman official if Pilate should let Jesus go. Jesus had defied the authority of the emperor.

The Pilate brought Jesus out in front of the people. Pilate said to the Jews, "Here is your king." Pilate coupled this action with a last effort to release Jesus. But the Jews blackmailed him again with the threat that he could be charged with high treason.

Pilate asked, "Shall I crucify your king?" The Jews replied that they had no king but Caesar. Pilate was a crafty politician, but he was a coward. He surrendered human feeling before the wrath of Jesus' enemies. He handed Jesus over to be crucified.

❏ *John 19:17-22.* John's account of the way to the cross and the Crucifixion is brief. John omits episodes that the other Gospels include, such as Simon of Cyrene's being pressed into service to carry Jesus' cross, Jesus' words to the women of Jerusalem, and the conversation of Jesus with the criminals on the cross. We have to remember, however, that John is mainly interested in a theological grasp of the material he includes. He wants to emphasize Jesus' humanity and its meaning.

"So the soldiers took charge of Jesus. Carrying his own cross, he went out to the place of the Skull (which in Aramaic is call Golgotha)." Notice that Jesus carried his own cross. He was going through no mock play. Jesus faced the agony of a criminal's death.

Crucifixion was possibly the most cruel and horrifying death to which a person could be subjected. The victim, bearing his own cross, was taken by a company of four Roman soldiers to the place of execution. There the victim was nailed to the cross and left to die. His corpse was left to be eaten by vultures. So horrible was crucifixion that it could not be used in Rome. It was used in lands subject to Rome and reserved for slaves. No Roman citizen could be crucified.

The procedure for crucifying a man never varied. When the criminal was condemned, the judge said, "You will go to the cross"; and the criminal was sent immediately to his death. The victim was often whipped on his way to the scene of execution. He and the company walked through as many streets as possible. Theirs was a very public spectacle, with an officer walking before the condemned one. The officer bore a placard on which was written the crime for which the man had been sentenced to death.

So the placard for Jesus' cross read: "Jesus of Nazareth, the King of the Jews." These words were written by Pilate in Aramaic, in Latin, and in Greek. Pilate's use of the three languages was appropriate, for the three languages would be needed in Jerusalem. Latin was the official tongue of the Roman government; Greek was the tongue of international trade; and Aramaic (a dialect of Hebrew) was the tongue of Palestinian Jews.

When the Jews objected to Pilate's words for the cross, Pilate refused to change them: "What I have written, I have written." John wants us to understand that Pilate had written his own record so far as acceptance or rejection of Jesus is concerned. That record cannot now be changed.

❑ *John 19:23-37.* The four soldiers at the cross did their jobs. Then they gambled for Jesus' clothing. Roman authorities permitted soldiers to keep the clothing of persons whom they crucified. Jesus, like every male Jew, wore five pieces of clothing—a headdress, an outer garment, shoes, a girdle, and a tunic. How could the soldiers divide the spoils of their service to the state?

CHRIST CRUCIFIED: "IT IS FINISHED"   **93**

The soldiers decided that each would take a piece of the apparel except for the tunic, which was a seamless garment. They did not want to tear the robe, so they decided to gamble for it. At the foot of the cross they threw dice to determine who would get the seamless tunic.

John suggests to us that the soldiers, missing the significance of their part in the great drama of salvation, unknowingly fulfilled the prophecy of Psalm 22:18.

This incident, which is just a minor episode in the eyes of the soldiers, thus carries deep meaning for the Gospel writer. It helps readers recognize the unconcern of the world over the salvation that God was working out for the whole world. The soldiers went about their business, unaware of the drama that was being enacted before them.

The soldiers were indifferent to the agonies of the Son of God, just as many of us have been callous to the pain and suffering of Jesus Christ, who is identified with "the least of these" among us: those who are ill, hungry, homeless, imprisoned, lonely, forsaken (Matthew 25:31-46).

John 19:25 tells us that four women stood near the cross of Jesus. They were his mother, his mother's sister, Mary the wife of Clopas, and Mary Magdalene. We know nothing about Mary the wife of Clopas, but we know a little about the others.

Jesus' mother's sister is not named in John's Gospel, but from a study of Mark 15:40 and Matthew 27:56 scholars are convinced that she was Salome, mother of James and John (Zebedee). Jesus had rebuked this woman when she came asking that her sons be given chief places in his kingdom (Matthew 20:20). Her presence at the cross indicates that she had taken Jesus' rebuke rightly and learned from it.

We know that Mary Magdalene was the woman out of whom Jesus had cast seven demons (Mark 16:9; Luke 8:2). Jesus' compassion had saved her from evil powers and prompted her loyalty in the hour of his death.

The story of Jesus' concern for his mother has always evoked interest among Christians. While the great drama of world salvation was being enacted, Jesus was protective of his mother. Christians should take this incident as one showing Jesus' practical concern and family loyalty. He was Mary's oldest son, and even on the cross he was thinking of what would happen to her.

Having entrusted Mary to John's care, Jesus then fulfills the Scripture (Psalm 69:21) with the words "I am thirsty" and the vinegar he is given to drink. He then utters a cry of victory: "It is finished." Jesus' cry says he has finished the work that God has sent him to earth to do. It is the shout of triumph such as an athlete would make on crossing the finish line. Jesus has lifted the cup of salvation on behalf of the world—on behalf of you and me. In the Incarnation, Jesus is fully human and fully divine. He is human enough to endure all our human sufferings. He is divine enough to reveal in our human life the very heart of God.

❏ *John 19:38-42.* Jesus died a criminal's death, but he had an honorable burial. Two secret disciples and members of the Sanhedrin—Joseph of Arimathea and Nicodemus—were responsible for this. Joseph went to Pilate and asked for Jesus' body so he could bury it. He provided a tomb for Jesus' body. Nicodemus gave the spices for Jesus' entombment. They followed the Jewish custom of wrapping the body of a dead person in fine linen cloths and of putting sweet spices inside the linen. Jesus' death brought out the splendor of his life and prompted the two men to declare openly their allegiance to him. Both showed great courage.

DIMENSION THREE:
WHAT DOES THE BIBLE MEAN TO ME?

What Shall We Do With Jesus?

We face the same question that Pilate faced: What shall I do with Jesus? Pilate wanted to keep his job, to succeed. He compromised and finally turned coward.

Pilate wanted to be his own God. In that ambition he confronted a temptation of us all. In our common, everyday speech we often hear an ambitious person say, "I want to be at the center of things." These words may carry different meanings to us. They may show a desire to manipulate others, to wield power, and to be involved. We are required to choose between Jesus and Pilate.

Pilate was satisfied with the world he had learned to manipulate. He wanted a world of his own making. Jesus' teachings would lead us to a world of God's making. A Christian is one who shares Christ's vision of the kingdom of God on earth. A Christian is one who shares in eternal life now and wants what Christ wants for society.

A Christian is one who realizes all power is ultimately from God, a reality that Pilate missed. Pilate cowered under the pressures of society. Do you, like Pilate, seek ways out of your responsibility when the going gets rough? Are you afraid of the power of public opinion?

What is the meaning of the Crucifixion for you personally? God comes to us in Jesus Christ teaching, working, sacrificing, suffering. "The word became flesh and made his dwelling among us." Your life now may be judged as forever precious.

Again Jesus said, "Peace be with you!
As the Father has sent me, I am sending you" (20:21).

—— 12 ——
Christ Is Risen!
John 20

DIMENSION ONE:
WHAT DOES THE BIBLE SAY?

Answer these questions by reading John 20

1. When does Mary Magdalene come to the tomb early and see that the stone "had been removed from the entrance"? (20:1)

2. When Mary runs from the tomb, whom did she meet? (20:2)

3. What does Mary say to them? (20:2)

4. Who outruns Peter to be the first disciple to reach the tomb? (20:4)

5. What do the other disciple and Peter see on reaching the tomb? (20:6-7)

6. What do the two disciples do? (20:8)

7. What does Mary do and see? (20:11-12)

8. What do the angels ask Mary, and what is Mary's reply? (20:13)

9. Whom does Mary now see, and what does he tell her? (20:14-17)

10. What is Mary's message to the disciples? (20:18)

11. What happens on the evening of the first day? (20:19-20a)

12. What is the response of the disciples to all this? (20:20b)

13. What does Jesus do and say next? (20:21-23)

14. What do the disciples tell Thomas when he arrives? (20:25a)

15. What is Thomas's reply? (20:25b)

16. What happens a week later? (20:26-27)

17. What is Thomas's response? (20:28)

18. What does Jesus say? (20:29)

19. What was John's purpose in writing the Gospel? (20:31)

DIMENSION TWO:
WHAT DOES THE BIBLE MEAN?

❑ *John 20:1-10.* We are often drawn to the scenes where we have met with great disappointments and defeats. We return to relive old sorrows—and perhaps to ask ourselves why life caved in there.

So when Mary Magdalene returned to the tomb of Jesus, she came in a dejected mood. Her hopes had been dashed. Where should she go now to find anything worth living for?

Jesus, the rare person of wisdom and compassion, was dead. Mary had seen his splendor. She had witnessed his redeeming love and had been able to receive it as her own. Now Jesus was gone. Mary, no doubt, was bitter. She experienced a mood of darkness.

Mary Magdalene was not afflicted with that vague malady we sometimes call "the blues." The whole meaning of her life was wrapped up in her experience at the tomb. The tomb meant the loss of hope, the coming of despair.

Mary came to the tomb on Easter Day while it was still dark. She saw the stone had been rolled away, so her first impulse was to share this information with others who would be concerned by it. She raced to meet Simon Peter and the other disciple. Mary said to them: "They have taken the Lord out of the tomb and we don't know where they have put him!" This is the most anguished cry in human experience. Mary thought somebody had stolen the body of Jesus. She had nothing left.

Peter and the other disciple (traditionally thought to be John) ran to the tomb. John, who was probably the younger of the two, reached the tomb first. Upon arrival, John stayed outside; but he peered into the tomb and saw the linen burial cloth. When Peter came, he entered the tomb and also saw the burial cloth lying as though Jesus' body had passed through the garments without disturbing their freshness and order. This description is this Gospel's way of indicating the reality of the Resurrection and the belief that would be stirred within the disciples.

❏ *John 20:11-18.* For the second time we hear Mary's cry of anguish: "They have taken my Lord away, . . . and I don't know where they have put him." It is a cry of bitter disappointment over what has happened to Jesus' body. Probing deeper into the Gospel's prose, we may find that Mary is expressing the mood of doubt and hopelessness that afflicts her and the people around her. Faith has fled, and now there seems no one to whom the people can turn for hope and support. Mary's mood expresses the cry for many modern people as well. A sense of great loss distresses them, a loss they cannot always define.

To this sense of loss the risen Christ speaks, so that Mary's experience becomes our own. When Mary sees the two angels (God's messengers), they ask her, "Woman, why are you crying?" Mary answers the angels. But from behind her Jesus speaks to her. God is present here, but he speaks beyond the questions of his messengers. Jesus is One especially sent.

Where is God in the hour of Mary's anguish? She has only to turn around to behold God in the person of Jesus Christ. John's Gospel has given us here a recognition scene wherein the Lord is made known.

Mary turns around. At first she mistakes Jesus for the gardener. Then the truth of the divine revelation confronts her. She says to Jesus in Hebrew, "Rabboni!" a word that means "Teacher" or "Master." Jesus cautions her not to hold on to him; for he has not yet ascended to the Father.

Mary has focused her attention too much on the tomb, not on the One who has left the tomb. Here we have a parable of Christians in every age. We become fascinated with the wrong aspect of the Resurrection, like the crusaders in the Middle Ages who bathed Europe and the Middle East in blood in Crusades intended to wrest the tomb of Jesus from the infidel. They forgot the message of Jesus that would seek justice, mercy, and love for all people. The crusaders knew they had a task assigned to them; but like many modern Christians, they misunderstood their task.

Mary knew her task. She was to go to Christ's brethren and say, "I have seen the Lord!" She responded at once.

"I have seen the Lord!"—that is what Christ tells us to say today. Christians have seen the Lord in a countless series of divine mercies and wonders—in personal sins forgiven, in persons being reconciled to God and to one another, in magnificent works of compassion, education, and healing. A Christian cannot contemplate the past or look out on the acts of God's steadfast love and not be moved to say, "I have seen the Lord." We have seen *the Word made flesh*. How can we fail to tell others about it?

❏ *John 20:19-23*. The disciples were now a frightened band, afraid to venture beyond the narrow confines of home. They knew Jesus' enemies were enemies of theirs because they had absorbed Jesus' understanding of life and of God's will. On Easter evening they had come together behind closed doors "for fear of the Jews." The disciples feared that the agents of the Sanhedrin might rap on their doors and take them prisoner.

Suddenly Jesus stood among them. He greeted them with the usual words: "Peace be with you!" With these words, Jesus conferred on the disciples his commission. It was a commission for the church and all Christians. Jesus told the disciples that as God had sent him to the world, so he was sending them. He had brought a message for all people, but now he was returning to the Father. He was leaving in the disciples' hands the ministry he had begun. He was leaving to the church the responsibility for proclaiming his message.

The disciples would not be left alone in their task. Jesus breathed on them and conferred on them the Holy Spirit. This action recalls the words from Scripture: "The LORD God formed the man from the dust of the ground and breathed into his nostrils the breath of life, and the man became a living being" (Genesis 2:7). The coming of the Holy Spirit suggests the raising of our life from the dead. Without the Holy Spirit, the church is lifeless.

Verse 23 has been much debated in Christian history. The promise that "If you forgive anyone his sins, they are forgiven; if you do not forgive them, they are not forgiven" does not mean that anyone can forgive another's sins. It means the church is granted the privilege of proclaiming the message of God's forgiveness to individuals. Having received the Holy Spirit, the church will be better able to understand the mind of God and better able to interpret God's forgiveness to people.

❏ *John 20:24-29.* Thomas was a pessimist, but he had his moments of bravery. When Jesus suggested going to Bethany, it was Thomas who said: "Let us also go, that we may die with him" (John 11:16). Thomas was loyal to Jesus—so much so that he was willing to give his life for the Master. Other disciples then were timid and afraid, but not so Thomas.

Thomas was a "loner," for he wanted to face his own grief over the Crucifixion in solitude. When the other disciples gathered behind closed doors for mutual support, Thomas was not there. He was in solitude with his sorrow over the death of Jesus.

Thomas had experienced the Crucifixion as death and defeat, so he could not believe the disciples when they said they had seen the Lord. Thomas had to be shown that Jesus had risen from the dead. He demanded the physical evidence—the print of the nails in Jesus' hands and the cut of the spear in Jesus' side.

A week later the disciples were gathered again. This time Thomas was present. He had been wrong to withdraw from the fellowship of the disciples the first time they assembled. Now he was present to see and hear for himself. He had been wrong to shut himself off from the concern and care of others. Many of us have been at fault in this attitude. We may have assumed that "nobody cares" or "my problems are too small to inflict upon anybody else" or "I don't want to be a burden to others."

To Thomas's credit, he returned to the fellowship. When he did come back into the fellowship, Thomas was absolutely honest about his stand. He came as "doubting Thomas," and he is remembered by this term today.

Thomas would not accept quick, simple answers to his doubts. God had given him intelligence, and his reason had to be satisfied. Thomas was not the type of Christian who turns off his mind when he enters the vestibule of faith. He would not accept easy, conventional answers to complex problems.

Thomas, moreover, was not a halfhearted Christian once he had seen and believed. He was wholehearted in his response to Christ: "My Lord and my God!" Doubt for Thomas was the great probing prelude to faith. And once he was convinced, he gave his life to the Master.

❑ *John 20:30-31.* John's Gospel contains no complete account of Jesus' earthly life. It was written that we may believe that "Jesus is the Christ, the Son of God," and that believing we may have life in his name.

John was familiar with the other three Gospels, and he used only the material from them that was essential to his purpose. Virtually all that Jesus did was a "sign"—a sign of God's way of dealing with us that we may have eternal life.

John's Gospel is not a biography of Jesus. John set out to tell us what God was doing through Jesus. We read this book rightly when we see it as John's help in our search for God.

DIMENSION THREE: WHAT DOES THE BIBLE MEAN TO ME?

A Meditation on the Risen Christ

Very early on Easter Day, Mary Magdalene stood in darkness and wept because "they have taken away my Lord" and she did not know where they had laid him. Mary experienced the pain and sorrow of a person when faith has gone and when Christ is reckoned as being dead. Mary experienced an overwhelming sense of futility and loss. Her experience may sometimes be our own.

But we, like Mary, have only to turn around when our name is called and to receive Christ into our lives. Mary at first did not recognize the risen Savior. How many times have we failed to recognize the resurrected One? He would make himself known in our daily experience—in mighty works, deeds of compassion, deeds of justice and mercy, deeds that compel us to behold him as Savior from hopelessness and despair.

"I am the way and the truth and the life. No one comes to the Father except through me" (John 14:6). He has shown us the way in Jesus Christ. God has revealed the truth about himself and us in the Man of Galilee. Jesus Christ has given vibrant, new life to all who have turned to him and all who have recognized his call.

The resurrected Savior gives us a task—a commission. Our task is to proclaim in our living that we have seen the Lord—seen the Lord in his ceaseless ministry to people in need. He lives!

Christ is risen! He raises us from our dead selves to be grasped by the Christian life in its wonder and beauty. Now we see human existence in the light of the Resurrection. Because Christ is risen, we are not alone in our commission. The Holy Spirit is in our lives, out in the world and in the fellowship of the church. We are social beings called to bear witness together to God's love supremely made known in Christ.

Today's lesson is a call to us to learn from the example of Thomas—Thomas "the loner" who returned to the fellowship of the disciples. Thomas insisted on a firsthand relationship with Jesus Christ. He wanted no secondhand religion. Thomas bids us across the centuries to be intelligent in our faith. He would teach us to search the Scriptures, to open our minds to what God is saying to us through them, and above all, to pray.

Jesus did many other things as well. If every one of them were were written down, I suppose that even the whole world would not have room for the books that would be written (21:25).

— 13 —

Victory and Christ's Call
John 21

DIMENSION ONE:
WHAT DOES THE BIBLE SAY?

Answer these questions by reading John 21

1. To whom does Jesus reveal himself by the Sea of Tiberias? (21:1-2)

2. What does Simon Peter say he is going to do, and what happens? (21:3)

3. Who is standing on the beach early the next morning? (21:4)

4. When he asks the disciples if they had caught any fish and receives a negative reply, what does Jesus tell them to do? (21:5-6a)

5. What do the disciples do then, and what results from their action? (21:6b)

6. Who first recognizes Jesus, and what does he say? (21:7a)

7. What does Peter do when he hears this? (21:7b)

8. What do the other disciples do? (21:8)

9. What do the disciples see when they get to land, and what does Jesus say to them? (21:9-10)

10. What does Peter do then, and what does Jesus say to the disciples? (21:11-12)

11. What is said after they finish breakfast? (21:15-19)

DIMENSION TWO: WHAT DOES THE BIBLE MEAN?

❏ *John 21:1-14.* Chapter 21 is an appendix to the Gospel of John. It is an epilogue, written to emphasize all that has been said in the Gospel.

The seven disciples are a discouraged group. They have seen Christ as he has revealed himself after the Resurrection. Now they are waiting, asking themselves what will happen next. Their existence is quiet, perhaps dull. Suddenly, Peter the impetuous one declares he is going fishing. He is returning to his old occupation where he will find some security. Six disciples tell him they will go with him. The seven fish all night, but they catch nothing.

Early the next morning they see Jesus standing on the beach, although they do not recognize him at first. He asks them, "Haven't you any fish?" They answer no. What is Jesus' response?

The risen Christ does not say, "I see you have been engaged in secular work. This is not preparation for the kingdom of God. Stop this nonreligious activity." No. The risen Christ sanctifies our work for all time when he says, "Throw your net on the right side of the boat." In other words, engage yourselves in the occupation in which you have been placed. What is your job in life? Homemaker? Farmer? Sanitation worker? Nurse? Clerk? Physician? Secretary? Carpenter? Lawyer? Technician? Electrician? Plumber? Public official? Teacher? Writer? Do this job to win your living—a living consecrated to the glory of God.

The risen Christ engaged himself in preparing breakfast for his disciples. He allowed these men to share the task with him, just as a good parent permits a child to do chores about the house. Everywhere John's Gospel puts emphasis on our physical and material existence. The Gospel stresses our human freedom and responsibility. God does not do everything for us. God maintains a providential order in which we are called to do for ourselves and to work for the divine creation. We are workers together with God. This fact gives to our work its dignity.

So Chapter 21 continues to combat what Amos N. Wilder called the "false spirituality" of the church, a spirituality that afflicts many Christians and their denominations today. This false spirituality is an escapism. It wants an escape hatch from involvement in the real world. It is a dualism, Wilder holds, that lodges Christian experience in the soul instead of in the whole person. Christian experience is found in the feelings rather than in the will. Such dividing of the human being into body and soul forgets that the individual is a unity of body, mind, and spirit.

We forget, Wilder says, that grace and revelation come to persons not through their heads and hearts, but through elemental factors in their human nature—that is, through the ordinary aspects of human existence, such as family relationships, patriotism, making a living, and growing old.

The dualism we practice, Wilder maintains, thrives on a misunderstanding of the Holy Spirit. Many Christians are inclined to see the Holy Spirit as a mood or a blessing "that has to do with the top story of our natures, and most often in detachment from life." But the Spirit does not separate us from life, does not speak only to the soul. The Spirit works in our total existence to energize and cleanse our creaturely and practical being. The Spirit involves all our human and moral relationships. Christians should affirm that the Holy Spirit "does not give us escape *from* this world but solutions *within* it."

Along with our misunderstanding of the Spirit goes our poor grasp of God's "Word"; for we see it as "a bolt from the blue or a light shining suddenly upon the soul." We often fail to acknowledge that the Word reaches us through our involvement with mundane and commonplace experience.

In the Bible, Wilder says, God reveals himself where people really live, in concrete situations, and to the whole person. Wilder concludes that "the Bible is a very human book and warns us against any kind of false spirituality." Revelation and God's grace are bound up inseparably with our bodily existence with all its organic relationships that reach out into the social, economic, and political areas of life. God does not short-circuit the original endowments of our human nature, and God does not disregard the ties that bind us "with nature, family and clan."[1]

Chapter 21 of the Fourth Gospel, then, picks up a theme of the whole Bible and warns us of the false spirituality that often plagues individuals and the church. The risen Christ has a way of making himself known in the work place and the marketplace, and there he confronts us daily.

VICTORY AND CHRIST'S CALL **109**

❏ *John 21:15-23.* After the disciples had eaten their breakfast, Jesus turned to Simon Peter, the obvious leader of the group, and asked, "Simon son of John, do you truly love me more than these?" Jesus may have pointed his hand toward the boat, its fishing gear, and its catch of fish when he asked his question. It was a question Jesus was asking the other disciples as well; for as their leader Peter represented them. In effect Jesus was asking Peter whether he was willing to give up his good job, with its rewards of plenty and promises of a fine career. Would he abandon all this for Jesus' mission, a mission that would involve great uncertainties, hardships, and even risks to Peter's life?

On the other hand, Jesus may have meant the disciples by referring to "these." He may have been asking Peter whether he loved his Lord more than he loved the other disciples. Jesus may also have been reminding Peter of the apostle's failure of nerve when he was questioned about being a follower of the Messiah.

However we interpret Jesus' question, it is clear that Jesus was pressing Peter to re-examine his purpose in life. Would Peter be a faithful advocate of the Christian mission? Would he accept for his own the purpose of Christ? Would he be motivated by love of Christ? Would Christ's call to be truly human take precedence over everything else?

Three times in the conversation Jesus asks Peter about his love and loyalty, and three times he gets Peter's answer. Three times Jesus tells Peter what he must do. Jesus first says, "Feed my lambs"—that is, feed Jesus' younger ones. Then he says, "Take care of my sheep." Finally, he says, "Feed my sheep." In other words, minister to my more mature people. Minister in love.

Jesus indicated that this ministry would bring Peter to his own cross. A strong Christian tradition holds that Peter was crucified in Rome. In love of Christ, Peter gave himself; he literally took up his cross and followed Christ. He became the foremost leader of the Christian community.

John 21:20-23 brings the beloved disciple into the conversation. Peter sees this disciple following Jesus and asks Jesus what will happen to John. But Jesus is not diverted by Peter's question. Look to yourself, Jesus tells Peter. What the Master does with the beloved disciple is no concern of Peter's. Peter's responsibility is to follow the Lord, not to speculate over the Lord's dealing with others.

❏ *John 21:24-25.* The beloved disciple is the disciple who now bears witness to the victory of Christ in the world. The beloved disciple has the reputation of giving accurate testimony to the truth of the gospel as it is recorded in this book. The church believes the message is true, but here in the Gospel of John only a small fraction of the story of Jesus can be told. The spread of the gospel of God in Jesus Christ is vast and endless, so that if all the reports of the gospel were to be written, "I suppose that even the whole world would not have room for the books that would be written."

DIMENSION THREE: WHAT DOES THE BIBLE MEAN TO ME?

The Christian Life Is a Victorious Life

Our lessons have dwelt on the themes of God's love of us and the world and what God does for us in Jesus Christ. Jesus in his death on the cross and his resurrection from the dead has conquered our chief enemies: sin and death. Christ calls us to accept the gracious gift of God, to accept God's forgiveness, and to accept all life relationships as a sacred trust.

This lesson appropriately deals with the risen Christ, how he dealt with the meaning of work, and our responsibilities for the world that God supremely loved.

Our Scripture would prompt us to ask some basic questions:

What is our purpose in life? Do we consider our work a sacred calling? Do we love Christ above all earthly things? Do we love the world as Christ loved it, no matter how ugly and despairing sin has made it?

Have the lessons helped us rethink our attitudes regarding life, its blessings, opportunities, and duties? Do we try to escape from responsible participation in life? How?

What is a false spirituality? How do you think Christians and the church are guilty of a false spirituality?

Do we seek escape from Jesus' call to the truly human life? How does the Holy Spirit operate in our existence? Do we seek detachment from this world rather than solutions within it? Explain your answer.

What was the call the risen Christ gave to Peter? How can we know who Christ's sheep are? What does it mean to feed Christ's sheep today?

---
[1] Quotations and paraphrases are from *Otherworldliness and the New Testament,* by Amos N. Wilder (Harper and Brothers, 1954); pages 17–37.